JOSSEY-BASS GUIDES
TO ONLINE TEACHING AND LEARNING

Exploring the Digital Library

A Guide for Online Teaching and Learning

Kay Johnson
and Elaine Magusin

JOSSEY-BASS
A Wiley Imprint
www.josseybass.com

Published by Jossey-Bass
A Wiley Imprint
989 Market Street, San Francisco, CA 94103-1741   www.josseybass.com

Jossey-Bass books and products are available through most bookstores. To contact Jossey-Bass directly call our Customer Care Department within the U.S. at 800-956-7739, outside the U.S. at 317-572-3986, or fax 317-572-4002.

Jossey-Bass also publishes its books in a variety of electronic formats. Some content that appears in print may not be available in electronic books.

Library of Congress Cataloging-in-Publication Data

Johnson, Kay, 1963-
  Exploring the digital library : a guide for online teaching and learning / Kay Johnson and Elaine Magusin.
    p. cm.
  Includes bibliographical references and index.
  ISBN-13: 978-0-7879-7627-9 (alk. paper)
  ISBN-10: 0-7879-7627-X (alk. paper)
  1. Digital libraries. 2. Academic libraries—Information technology. 3. Academic libraries—Relations with faculty and curriculum. 4. Electronic information resource literacy—Study and teaching (Higher) 5. Information literacy—Study and teaching (Higher) 6. Libraries and distance education. 7. Scholarly electronic publishing. 8. Digital libraries—Canada—Case studies. I. Magusin, Elaine. II. Title.
  ZA4080.J64 2005
  025'.00285--dc22   2005009301

Printed in the United States of America

FIRST EDITION

PB Printing   10 9 8 7 6 5 4 3 2 1

Contents

To Neil and Tristan (Kit), and to Jim for all the books.

K. J.

For Mum, Dad, and Heather.

E. M.

Preface

Rapid advances in telecommunications and computer networks are altering the landscape of everyday life. E-mail, search engines, virtual realities, hypertextuality, cyberpunk, and the dot-coms have entered our lives. We live in an age in which governments, economic systems, social services, mass media—the very foundations of contemporary society—are plugged in to digital technology. This is not to say that our long heritage of print culture is no longer vital, but we are in the midst of a distinctive digital culture. As Charlie Gere, author of *Digital Culture,* observes: "Digitality . . . encompasses both the artefacts and the systems of signification and communication that most clearly demarcate our contemporary way of life from others" (2002, p. 12).

The advent of the Internet, the World Wide Web, electronic publishing, and digital libraries is having a tremendous impact on teaching, learning, and scholarship. New relationships, processes, and issues emerge with the ability to access worldwide digital collections from one's desktop, to exchange ideas and data with colleagues around the globe almost instantaneously, and to publish in multimedia formats. Widespread use of information and communication technologies (ICTs) has led to a growth in distance and online learning and a redefinition of the academic library.

Digital technology is transformational and transformations lead to complex human reactions. The range of responses run the gamut from the techno-whiz who embraces computers wholeheartedly and unquestioningly, to the modern-day Luddite who cautions that nothing good can come of this new machinery. In general, most of us have adapted to computers. We have learned the programs we need to know to complete our work and to amuse ourselves. The problem that we face is that with so many programs, so many ways of interacting with computers, and so many virtual spaces in which to seek out information, it is easy to become completely overwhelmed.

This is not a "how to build a digital library" book; instead, it is an exploration of digital libraries and digital library culture. When we speak of *digital library culture* we are drawing from anthropological concepts to illuminate the obstacles that users may experience in interacting with a digital library. Cultural barriers, such as not knowing the language, norms, or customs of a group, can impede understanding. Digital libraries, in addition to having a distinct culture, are characterized by diversity and by change. Searchers face a multiplicity of systems, interfaces, search protocols, and hyperlinked paths. It is easy to get stumped, dazzled, or just lost and bewildered in the electronic labyrinth. As information vendors compete in the marketplace, systems get new looks and other enhancements so that the system you know today may not be exactly the same as the one you log in to tomorrow.

Our experiences as distance librarians at Athabasca University (AU) inform much of what we have written here. Founded in 1970, AU is known as Canada's Open University, a distance education university dedicated to the removal of barriers that restrict access to higher learning. Historically, the university has relied on the fixtures of traditional distance education, such as print-based course packages, contact with tutors by toll-free telephone, and use of the postal system. These methods continue today. But since the 1990s the university, along with distance education postsecondary institutions everywhere, has been working to incorporate online technologies in a manner that is cost-effective, is competitive with other institutions offering online courses, and provides students with a high-quality and flexible learning experience. University and departmental Web pages, learning management systems, e-mail correspondence, computer-mediated communication systems, electronic databases, and digital libraries are some of the new fixtures of distance education as well as of traditional universities as they too venture into online education.

Whether they are involved in distance education or teach on traditional campuses, faculty are increasingly expected to be fluent not only in print culture but in digital culture, and to ensure that their students are fluent as well. This book provides opportunities for faculty to explore the nature of digital libraries and digital library use in higher learning. A broad spectrum of competencies goes into the making of a digital scholar who is capable not only of using digital libraries effectively but of contributing to the scholarly online environment. The symbiotic relationship in which libraries serve the research needs of scholars and in which scholars write the publications that libraries acquire, manage, and provide access to makes a discussion of electronic scholarly communication crucial to our treatment of digital library culture. We offer models for faculty to integrate digital culture into their professional lives, to collaborate in the development of digital libraries, to use online resources to enhance the learning experiences of their students, and to participate in online scholarly communities. Librarians who are seeking to build collaborative relationships with faculty and to promote information literacy and digital scholarship in their institutions will benefit from discussion of these topics, as will university and college administrators and those responsible for faculty development.

Chapter One seeks a cultural understanding of the digital library. We look at the development of digital libraries, transformations in academic libraries, and cultural barriers to successful digital library use.

In Chapter Two we discuss how information and communication technologies, and electronic publishing in particular, are transforming scholarly communication. This brings many opportunities to disseminate ideas and to be creative with media, but there are issues pertaining to the acceptance of electronic publication in the promotion, tenure, and review process.

Chapter Three provides suggestions for faculty to integrate digital libraries into their teaching and course development, so that students have contextual, seamless access to online library resources and services. Faculty play an important role in promoting library use to their students and have an opportunity to model a relationship with the digital library that students can be encouraged to emulate.

In Chapter Four we describe approaches to promoting information literacy skills, and most importantly, integrating these skills across the curriculum. Information literacy is sometimes seen as the responsibility of the library; the reality is that for information literacy initiatives to be truly successful, faculty involvement is crucial.

Chapter Five considers the skills and knowledge required in digital library use. An understanding of principles common to information systems enables searchers to move beyond dependence on a few key systems and strategies and toward a deeper comprehension of information retrieval. The information-seeking behaviors of faculty and students are changing in response to the availability of electronic resources. Access to scholarly and unique digital collections should be increasing the breadth of information resources available to students, yet many instructors find themselves struggling with the poor quality of work their students are turning in. We explore some key challenges that faculty and librarians are facing, including plagiarism and overreliance on limited digital collections.

Chapter Six focuses on the topic of collaboration as we consider opportunities for faculty and librarians to work together in the online educational environment. Collaboration between faculty and librarians, as well as other institutional stakeholders, ensures that the academic digital library meets the needs of its community. This chapter is followed by two case study chapters, in which we use our projects at AU to illustrate models for collaboration.

Chapter Seven looks at how AU librarians and faculty are working together to promote information literacy skills. Chapter Eight focuses on AU's collaboratively developed enhanced electronic course reserves system, the Digital Reading Room (DRR). The DRR provides opportunities to share and reuse learning resources, and we consider how the development and use of learning objects is a growing trend in education.

Chapter Nine concludes our book by addressing the question: "Does using a digital library get easier?" Overcoming digital library cultural barriers enables academics, and other digital library users, to become active contributors to worldwide digital repositories of knowledge. To be a successful digital library user it is necessary to understand the culture and have the skills to access, retrieve, evaluate, and use digital information. This will not change, but there are developments that promise to make the online environment a friendlier place.

Acknowledgments

I would like to thank all of the faculty, staff, and students at Athabasca University who have helped me develop as a distance librarian by sharing their insights into what it means to teach and learn, and provide student support, in a distance learning community. A special thank-you goes to members of the INFS 200 course development team—Jeremy Mouat, Billy Cheung, Ian Grivois, and John Ollerenshaw—who demonstrate what collaboration is all about, and to Susan Moisey who responded so quickly to a last-minute request for a paper.

K. J.

I would like to thank all the people who provided assistance and support to me in the writing process and let me talk endlessly about this project. Special thanks go to Gilda Sanders, Geoff Peruniak, and Vincent Ambrock, who answered my questions. Your assistance proved invaluable.

E. M.

About the Authors

Kay Johnson is head of Reference and Circulation Services, Library Services, Athabasca University.

Johnson received Bachelor of Arts degrees in English and history from the University of Ottawa and a Master of Library and Information Studies from McGill University. She has been with Athabasca University since 2000, working with students and faculty to make sense of online information, contributing to the development of the library's digital gateway to resources and services, and coauthoring and tutoring the AU course INFS 200: Accessing Information. She has presented at the Eleventh Off-Campus Library Services Conference (2004), the Nineteenth Annual Conference on Distance Teaching and Learning (2003), and the ICDE/CADE North America Regional Distance Education Conference (2002). Johnson is a contributing author to *Theory and Practice of Online Learning*, published by Athabasca University and available to readers online at no cost.

Elaine Magusin is a reference services librarian with Library Services, Athabasca University.

Magusin holds a Bachelor of Arts in music from the University of British Columbia and a Master of Library and Information Science from the University of Western Ontario. She has focused her career on providing reference and bibliographic instruction services to patrons in a variety of environments, including government, public, and academic libraries. Prior to joining Athabasca University Library she worked as a music reference librarian in the Boston Public Library's Research Library.

Magusin's recent publications include "Library Services: Designing the Digital Reading Room to Support Online Learning" in *Proceedings from the 19th Annual Conference on Distance Teaching and Learning* (Madison: Board of Regents of the University of Wisconsin System, 2003) and "Collaborating on Electronic Course Reserves to Support Student Success," in Patrick B. Mahoney (Ed.), *Eleventh Off-Campus Library Services Conference Proceedings* (Mount Pleasant: Central Michigan University, 2004).

Digital Libraries:
A Cultural Understanding

In the novel *Galapagos,* Kurt Vonnegut has one of his characters invent a device called "Mandarax." This pocket computer not only functions as a simultaneous voice translator but can diagnose 1,000 common human diseases, teach the delicate art of flower arranging, and display on command any one of the 20,000 popular quotations stored in its memory. Mandarax is eventually marooned on a remote island for 31 years with the last 10 human survivors on earth. The Captain destroys it in a final rage at its useless knowledge and failure to make sense of information, not to mention its little beeping sounds: "As the new Adam, it might be said, his final act was to cast the Apple of Knowledge into the deep blue sea" (Vonnegut, 1985, p. 62).

As an apple of knowledge, digital technology has tremendous potential. It has altered the way people access, use, create, distribute, and store information, and it has had a far-reaching impact on almost all facets of society. Yet it seems to be in the very nature of computers to rankle and try the patience of the human beings who use them. Often one may, like Vonnegut's angry Captain, want to cast the apple out to sea. It is in active roles—as participants, contributors, and informed critics—that it is possible for us to make sense of digital information and help build a global digital repository of useful knowledge. This chapter seeks to define what we mean by *digital library*, looks at how the academic library is changing to meet the needs of distance learners and remote users, and considers cultural barriers to effective digital library use.

DIGITAL LIBRARIES IN THE MATRIX OF DIGITAL CULTURE

In considering digital libraries and their role in higher education, it is important to keep in mind that they represent only one component of the broader digital environment. Digital technology is all around us, and extends far beyond the most obvious emblem, the personal computer. From DVDs and wristwatches to banking systems and electricity grids, humanity is increasingly reliant on digital technology.

Technically, the word *digital* refers to the binary digits, the zeroes and ones, that represent data manipulated and stored by a computer. The term is more broadly used to refer to anything relating to computers. It is often said that this is the digital age, a statement that conveys the extent to which computers and technology are pervasive.

Since the introduction of relatively affordable personal computers and the development of the Internet and the World Wide Web, increasing numbers of individuals are using computers at work, school, and home. In September 2001 the Department of Commerce's Census Bureau found that 50.5% of U.S. households had an Internet connection (National Telecommunications and Information Administration and the Economics and Statistics Administration, 2002a). There has been a dramatic rise in household Internet access in other nations as well (Organization for Economic Co-operation and Development, 2002). Internet use is spreading into everyday life, with 88% of online Americans reporting that the Internet plays a role in their daily routines, such as communicating with family and friends and looking up information (Pew Internet & American Life Project, 2004). Today's mass media is bursting with excitement about such things as the "knowledge economy" and the "information society," indicating further the extent to which information and communication technologies have penetrated almost everywhere. Of course, where there are haves, there are also have-nots. There is the gap between the "information rich" and the "information poor," and various organizations are working to bridge the digital divide—to address inequities in the ability to access and effectively use information technologies.

The digital environment extends beyond technological issues. Gere identifies a digital culture that has emerged out of a complex set of interactions among elements such as "nineteenth-century capitalism, twentieth-century warfare, the postwar avant-garde, the counter-culture, post-modern theory and Punk," revealing digital culture to be not merely a product of technology but rather part of a cultural continuum (2002, p. 15). Digital culture influences not only the production and distribution of music, film, literature, and art but even the themes of our cultural products.

Libraries have traditionally represented a culture of the book, and call up for many the tactile associations of pages, bindings, and dust jackets. Libraries have been places of quiet reflection, inquiry, and sustained reading. They not only are timeless and comforting in a too-hectic world but also have preserved the human record through the ages. At the same time, libraries have entered the information superhighway and have come to represent digital culture as much as book culture.

DEFINING DIGITAL LIBRARIES

The antecedents of the digital library can be found in the writings of Vannevar Bush and J.C.R. Licklider. In a 1945 issue of *The Atlantic Monthly*, Dr. Bush envisioned the development of a device that he called the "memex," a mechanized system based on microfilm technology used to store, search, and display humanity's knowledge. In *Libraries of the Future* (1965), Licklider took the concept further and crafted the vision of a computer-based library. Librarians were early adopters of computers, with library automation beginning in the 1950s in the form of punched cards. Printed catalogue cards were replaced by machine-readable cataloguing format (MARC), which made it easier for librarians to share cataloguing data. Librarians converted their card catalogues to online public access catalogues (OPACs) and began using computers to manage the circulation of materials to borrowers. When the online information retrieval industry was in its early years librarians became expert searchers, using terminals to access remote computers to conduct information searches on behalf of library users. Librarians purchased indexes and other information products on CD-ROM to enhance their collections. With the development of the World Wide Web, and the move in the online industry to

Windows-based, mouse-driven graphical user interfaces, librarians began designing Web sites to manage and provide remote access to online collections.

Librarians have been "digital" for some time, but it was not until the 1990s that the subject of digital libraries began to receive significant attention. A growing number of journal and monograph publications as well as conferences are devoted to the topic, and initiatives have grown up around research and development. The Digital Library Federation (http://www.diglib.org/), founded in 1995, is a consortium of American academic libraries, the British Library, and other agencies that are "pioneering in the use of electronic-information technologies to extend their collections and services" (Digital Library Federation, 2005, para. 2). Chowdhury and Chowdhury (2002) outline some of the major global initiatives, which include the Digital Libraries Initiative, Phase 1 (http://www.dli2.nsf.gov/dlione/) and Phase 2 (http://www.dli2.nsf.gov/) in the United States, the Electronic Libraries (eLib) Programme in the United Kingdom (http://www.ukoln.ac.uk/services/elib/), the Delos Network of Excellence on Digital Libraries (http://delos-noe.iei.pi.cnr.it/), and the Canadian Initiative on Digital Libraries (http://www.collectionscanada .ca/cidl/). Academic Info (http://www.academicinfo.net/digital.html) provides a directory of digital library collections and resources, organized by subject.

Digital library projects are spread around the globe and present a diverse experience of what is meant by a digital library. Consider the digital libraries described in Exhibit 1.1. Each varies in the communities it serves, its purpose, the material formats and subject areas it includes, and many other aspects, yet each may still be called a digital library.

ACM Digital Library, the Cuneiform Digital Library Initiative, and the New Zealand Digital Library are purely digital libraries. However, many, such as the California Digital Library (CDL), are frequently found as components in hybrid library models that provide access to online resources and services to both on-site and remote users while at the same time providing users with access to physical resources housed in library buildings. CDL is a University of California library and collaborates with and assists UC campuses and their libraries.

The Library of Congress is the world's largest library, holding millions of physical objects, such as books, manuscripts, drawings, sound recordings, and films. Not surprisingly, the Library of Congress Web site functions as a gateway to search the vast physical collections using online catalogues. Although the digital collections make up only a fraction of its holdings, the Library of Congress offers an

Exhibit 1.1. A Sampling of Digital Libraries

Digital Library	Description
ACM Digital Library	*Organization:* Association for Computing Machinery. *Community:* ACM members have unlimited full-text access. The general public has access to the bibliographic database. *Purpose:* To provide access to ACM publications. *Contents:* Citations and full text of ACM journal and newsletter articles and conference proceedings. *URL:* http://www.acm.org/dl/
California Digital Library (CDL)	*Organization:* University of California. *Community:* Open to the public, but licensed resources are available only to the university's community. *Purpose:* "Supports the assembly and creative use of the world's scholarship and knowledge for the UC libraries and the communities they serve" (CDL, 2005, para. 1). *Contents:* Includes electronic journals, reference databases, government information, electronic books, archival images and documents, and the online catalogue. *URL:* http://www.cdlib.org/
Cuneiform Digital Library Initiative (CDLI)	*Organization:* A joint project of the University of California Los Angeles and the Max Planck Institute for the History of Science, funded by the Digital Libraries Initiative. *Community:* Open to the public, but primarily of interest to scholars and specialists. *Purpose:* "To make available through the internet the form and content of cuneiform tablets dating from the beginning of writing, ca. 3200 B.C., until the end of the third millennium" (CDLI, 2004, para. 1). *Contents:* Text and images, including document transliterations, text glossaries, and digitized originals and photo archives of early cuneiform. *URL:* http://cdli.ucla.edu/

(Continued)

Exhibit 1.1. A Sampling of Digital Libraries (Continued)

Digital Library	Description

Library of Congress	*Organization:* Library of Congress.
	Community: Open to the public.
	Purpose: To provide a gateway to the digital and nondigital collections of the Library of Congress.
	Contents: Includes LC online catalogues and other library catalogues, historical digital collections, legislative information, and digitized photographs.
	URL: http://www.loc.gov/
	    Digital Collections & Programs:
	    http://www.loc.gov/library/libarch-digital.html

New Zealand Digital Library	*Organization:* University of Waikato. *Community:* Open to the public. *Purpose:* Originated as a research project at the University of Waikato "to develop the underlying technology for digital libraries and make it available publicly so that others can use it to create their own collections" (2000, para. 1). Uses Greenstone digital library software. *Contents:* Humanitarian and UN collections and example collections including text, images and music. *URL:* http://www.nzdl.org/ fast-cgi-bin/library?a=p&p=home

impressive digital library. American Memory (http://memory.loc.gov) is the "flagship" of the library's digital collections, providing access to millions of digitized documents, photographs, sound recordings, motion pictures, and text from the American historical collections of the library and other institutions. THOMAS (http://thomas.loc.gov/) is the entry point for full-text legislative information, bills, and congressional records. Digital images accompany most of the records in the library's Prints and Photographs Online Catalog (http://www.loc.gov/rr/print/catalog.html). The Global Gateway (http://international.loc.gov/intldl/intldlhome.

html) links to international digital library collaborations and to the library's digital collections focusing on history and cultures around the world. The library also offers an "Ask a Librarian" e-mail–based reference service.

What the libraries shown in the exhibit all do is provide access to organized collections of information resources in digital format that users are able to access over an electronic network. Numerous definitions of digital libraries appear in the literature, and this can cause some confusion. It may help to offer the observations of Christine L. Borgman, who has identified two main streams in digital library definitions. One stream represents a technical focus and is put forward primarily by digital library researchers. Their emphasis is on "digital libraries as content collected on behalf of user communities." Generally, these definitions include technological capabilities such as methods for creation, organization, maintenance, and access and retrieval of information collections. The other stream identified by Borgman addresses the practical challenges of transforming library institutions, and is advanced by librarians who focus on "digital libraries as institutions or services" (1999, p. 229).

Borgman notes a third usage of the term that, for the most part, falls outside of the research and library communities' definitions. These are the Web sites, online databases, and CD-ROM products that identify themselves as digital libraries. The extent to which these electronic collections are organized, or designed for specific user communities, varies. Our concern here is primarily with the digital library as an extension of the academic research library. However, when we address digital library culture we are mindful that faculty and students encounter diverse types of digital libraries in their research activities. These electronic information collections may or may not be associated with a library.

All types of libraries are applying online technologies to their resources and services. Synonyms for the digital library include *virtual library, electronic library,* and *library without walls.* As the growth of electronic networks became a hot topic in the library literature in the early 1990s, D. Kaye Gapen defined the virtual library as "the concept of remote access to the contents and services of libraries and other information resources, combining an on-site collection of current and heavily used materials in both print and electronic form, with an electronic network which provides access to, and delivery from, external worldwide library and commercial information and knowledge sources" (1993, p. 1). It is this type of library—a hybrid of the print and the digital, including a gateway to online resources that extends the library collection beyond its physical walls—that researchers most frequently encounter in academic libraries today.

TRANSFORMING THE ACADEMIC LIBRARY

Academic libraries usually use their Web sites as gateways to various online resources that include research databases, library catalogues, electronic books, electronic journals, electronic course reserves, selected Web sites, and locally developed digital collections. Some of these resources are made available on the basis of licensing and are restricted to faculty, students, and staff associated with the institution; others are freely and publicly available. Some of the digital resources may be full-text versions of print equivalents; others are "born digital," existing in electronic form only. Some may be digital surrogates, records that represent the physical items that are accessible through the library's holdings or from other library collections. Exhibit 1.2 lists the main categories of physical and digital materials students or faculty members can expect to access through their academic library.

Significant changes are taking place in the academic library in response to available technologies, the needs and wants of remote users, and the increasing popularity of distance and online learning. William Y. Arms tells us, "The fundamental reason for building digital libraries is a belief that they will provide better delivery of information than was possible in the past" (2000, p. 4). Researchers can access a digital library anytime and anywhere that the necessary technology is available. A digital library delivers to the user's desktop not only bibliographic data about library collections and journal publications but also abstracts and full-text documents. It can link researchers to unique collections and archives from all over the world. Digital libraries are capable of delivering services as well as information. A digital library user may take an online library orientation or tutorial, renew materials online, use e-mail to request particular materials or services, or interact with librarians in real time using chat-based reference services.

For colleges and universities whose students and professors meet on-site, remote access to the library from home or work offers a flexible, convenient approach to accessing library services and resources. As traditional institutions expand their programs to incorporate distance and online learning, the digital library is becoming an increasingly important component in the support they offer their students. For distance education institutions and virtual universities, digital libraries

Exhibit 1.2. Physical and Digital Materials in the Academic Library

Physical materials (books, maps, videos, and so on):

- Physical items housed in the library
- Physical items available from other library collections through interlibrary loan
- Physical items borrowed from other libraries through reciprocal borrowing arrangements

Digital materials:

- Digital surrogates, or records that represent physical items—for example, the bibliographic records in the library's online catalogue or citations in a research database
- Digital resources that are derived from nondigital materials—for example, the electronic version of a journal for which there is a print publication
- Born-digital materials that exist in digital form only and for which there are no print equivalents—for example, a journal that is electronic only

are a significant element in their ability to provide their learning communities with "library services and resources equivalent to those provided for students and faculty in traditional campus settings" (Association of College & Research Libraries, 2004, para. 12). Digital libraries offer flexible approaches to delivering library materials and course reserves anywhere in the world. Many of the resources required to support university-level studies are not available digitally, but the number, depth, and scope of scholarly resources available online is improving as demand for electronic access increases. Communication tools such as e-mail, chat, and discussion boards enhance interactions among distance librarians, faculty, and students. Web-based forms streamline processes for requesting materials and services from libraries. Digital library users also benefit from the online search tutorials developed by librarians.

In the United States, distance education course enrollments at the undergraduate and graduate levels increased from 1.7 million to 3.1 million between 1997–98 and 2000–01. In 2000–01, 56% of all postsecondary institutions offered distance education courses, compared to 34% three years earlier (National Center for

Education Statistics, 2004, para. 2–3). A picture of the range of distance and online learning options available worldwide can be had by visiting some of the online education directories available on the Web, such as World Wide Learn (http://www.worldwidelearn.com/) and Peterson's Distance Learning (http://www.petersons.com/distancelearning/), and the Web sites of organizations such as the International Council for Open and Distance Education (http://www.icde.org/).

The roles of academic libraries are changing to meet new needs in higher education. The collection of books, manuscripts, and other physical materials continues to be important, but acquisition of resources in digital form involves a shift from ownership to access. Much of this digital content is not owned by the library but is made accessible on the basis of licensing agreements negotiated with publishers and vendors. This changes the library's relationship to its collection, with a significant loss of control over how material is organized and accessed, and in the case of bundled resources, over what is added or removed or duplicated in the collection.

Librarians' roles are also changing, as librarians are increasingly required to offer technical support to users accessing online libraries and to provide instruction in locating and using electronic information resources. The reference and instructional services that librarians traditionally provide are being transformed by an absence of face-to-face interaction as e-mail and chat are used more and more to connect with remote users. Librarians are responding in creative ways to the need to support learners and faculty in an online environment. There has been a dramatic rise in publication on the subject, which, as Alexander Slade and Marie Kascus note, reflects the changing role of the library and "the convergence of on- and off-campus library services as the electronic era blurs the boundaries between conventional and distance education and between remote and in-person users of libraries" (2000, p. xiv).

Digital culture has penetrated libraries to the effect that the future of the traditional library has come into question. It is true that in many cases information that was once accessed through the library may now be found on a Web site and the library can be bypassed altogether. What can be found through a search engine, however, can hardly be said to meet the full requirements of a scholarly approach to research and inquiry. Digital libraries are gateways to scholarly materials that have been selected by librarians and academics, and they have the power to connect researchers to librarians who offer personalized assistance and instruction. In *The Enduring Library,* Michael Gorman writes of the harmonious integration of digital technology into libraries: "Digital media will find their place and level in society and will be incorporated into the ever-evolving library" (2003, p. 31).

Digital culture often fails to address human concerns, resulting in feelings of anxiety, alienation, and frustration. These feelings can easily be carried over into interactions with digital libraries. Just as we can speak of digital culture, we can speak of a distinct digital library culture. In the next section we will discuss some of the challenges of acculturation to digital libraries.

DIGITAL LIBRARY CULTURE

Digital libraries are not just about online systems and their contents but also about the humans who interact with them. Concepts from the social sciences can help us understand this interaction. When anthropologists discuss culture they consider aspects such as norms, customs, language, and knowledge that help define a particular group of people. A traditional library has a culture that frequent library users take for granted but that could be a barrier for someone who has never stepped into a library before. There are systems for organizing knowledge, such as the Library of Congress classification system. There are social norms: it may seem polite to return to the shelves the books you have finished reading, but this seems to make the librarian angry. There is certainly a language in the form of librarian speak: *serial, access point,* and *authority control,* to just barely touch the surface. Digital libraries also have a distinct culture that relates to the need to learn new technologies but extends to new ways of thinking about information and new ways of interacting with libraries and with documents. Digital library culture poses some unique challenges for those on the way to becoming successful digital library users.

Disintermediation

Disintermediation is "one of the defining characteristics of digital libraries" (Chowdhury & Chowdhury, 2002, p. 284). In the early days of online information retrieval, when searchers had to learn command languages that varied from system to system and there were costly charges for connect times, librarians often functioned as intermediaries between the information seeker and the information system. This has largely given way to an era of databases available through fixed-cost subscriptions and intended for end-user searching, in which the information seeker interacts directly with the system. Because the searcher has remote access to the online databases, a librarian is usually not present to offer assistance. Given the ubiquity of digital technology, users of academic libraries can generally be expected to be familiar with computers, but this does not necessarily translate into an ability to search databases effectively. Depending on the complexity of the information need, the searcher may need to access, select from, and search a wide array of databases, formulate queries using a variety of search terms and search techniques, interpret search results appropriately, and refine searches as needed.

Talking to the Machine

In a traditional library, a library user may have difficulty understanding how a librarian communicates information queries and approaches information seeking. A librarian may have as much difficulty understanding the knowledge and terminology that the user brings to an academic discipline. However, the librarian and the library user are using human language (we will assume it is a language that they share), which, apart from all of its subtleties and imprecision, allows for negotiation and clarification of what information is needed—a process that librarians call the *reference interview.* When a machine joins the exchange, the process is complicated as librarians and library users find themselves interacting with a third party that has a language and set of protocols of its own. In many cases, digital library users interact directly with the machine, without a librarian's intervention, and find themselves in conversation with a computer that refuses to understand or cooperate. What a machine brings to the reference conversation is an impersonal, constricted language constructed out of controlled vocabulary terms and a grasp of human meaning generally limited to keyed-in characters, Boolean logic, and system commands.

The digital library also brings with it new language, which can end up sounding like a bunch of techno-babble and glitzy electronic jargon. There is the language associated with accessing and searching online library resources, such as *proxy server, wild card,* and *proximity operator.* As scholars communicate, teach, and publish online, they deal not only with intellectual content but also with digital technology. In contributing to digital repositories faculty find themselves dealing with *digital objects,* the items that are stored in a digital library, such as online journal articles or Web pages, and describing these objects with *metadata*—data about data. In order to create stable links to online articles from their pages, academics need to know how to build *PURLs,* the persistent uniform resource locators that take students directly to the online article regardless of any changes in the item's location on the Web over time. Through such activities, the language of digital libraries begins to enter academic language.

Fast-Paced Change

Traditional libraries change, but the pace of change is fairly slow, giving users time to learn how to deal with it. Digital libraries change quickly, requiring those who use them to relearn on a regular basis. Even experienced users of digital libraries find themselves challenged to keep up with the multiplicity of online products and the many updates and facelifts these products undergo. Digital libraries require ongoing adaptation to change because the very nature of online resources is dynamic.

Information Overload

The number of links, resources, and services available through a library Web site can easily overwhelm students and faculty. Easy-to-find and well-designed menus, site maps, and search engines can help with navigation, but there are still so many possibilities from which to choose. It is not always easy to see where the library site ends and nonlibrary resources and services begin. Yet digital libraries can also actually decrease information overload in a time when far too many students are basing their research papers on the first twenty items retrieved by a search engine query that produced 250,000 results. Digital libraries help searchers frame their query in the context of scholarly publications, links selected by librarians and academics, and resources organized by discipline.

Technostress

Computers can cause feelings of isolation and dehumanization, and make their users feel harried and hurried: the blinking cursor, the dinging sound when another e-mail message hits the in-box, and the error message that tells nothing. Increasing numbers of people are using computers, but even those who are highly experienced can feel *technostress.* Craig Brod popularized the term in 1984, defining it as "a modern disease of adaptation caused by an inability to cope with the new computer technologies in a healthy manner" (pp. 16–17). Kupersmith (1998) observes: "This effect can be quite subtle, as when people attempt to match their thinking and behavior to that of computer systems, especially when the interface design does little to adapt the underlying functions of the machine to human perceptions and behavior" (p. 26). Kupersmith considers some of the digital library challenges that may cause library users to experience technostress:

- The physical library building is fairly easy to find, but there can be challenges in finding and accessing a digital library.

- Once you enter a digital library you encounter multiple systems to search and may not always be aware of the systems' capabilities, or what might be the best system to search for a particular purpose.

- Once you are in an online system you may encounter an unfamiliar interface, commands, error messages, and terminology, because each system is different.

Fluency in Print and Digital Formats

Rigorous searching skills are required to access, retrieve, and interpret information effectively in an online environment; however, the bulk of humanity's most valuable scholarly material is not available in digital format. Today's scholars are expected to be comfortable with both digital culture and print (or book) culture. It helps to be aware of the characteristics of each in their authority, accessibility, flexibility, longevity, and the more elusive quality that we will call "personality."

Authority

Electronic documents can be published by anyone with access to a computer, Internet account, and Web-authoring software, so it is often difficult to determine the identity and subject expertise of the author. Yet electronic publication can mean different things, and it does not make sense to lump together an electronically published peer-reviewed journal and a high school student's assignment posted on a Web site. The same standards of print publication, such as editorial or peer review, can be applied to electronic publication.

Accessibility

Print culture in libraries is based on ownership of physical items. If all copies of a physical item are signed out, or the library is closed, you are out of luck. Yet a book, once you have a copy, is very portable and you do not need equipment to read it.

With the appropriate technology on hand, an electronic document is accessible anytime and anywhere, providing for convenient and quick access. Most electronic resources support multiuser access models. Accessibility is a complex issue when licensing is involved. In one sense, information is seen as being available anytime and anywhere through networks; in another sense, online accessibility can be severely curtailed by institutional privileges. In the academic library as building, a scholar can walk into most academic libraries in North America and access the print collection and the online databases as an on-site user. In the digital library, a scholar's remote access to resources is based on the library's licensing agreements and the scholar's institutional affiliation with the library. A researcher sending colleagues at another institution a link to an article in a database may find that they are unable to access the content if their institutions are not also subscribers (Borgman, 2000a; Lynch, 2003a).

Flexibility

It is possible to make notes on them, photocopy them, and lend them out, but for the most part paper documents are static. Digital documents are highly flexible. As electronic files, or hyperlinks, they are easy to share. If the font is too tiny it is easy to alter it. A search tool can scan through every word in an electronic text and retrieve occurrences of that word. Works in digital form are easy to update and revisions are fairly painless. However, malleability can be as much a concern as a benefit when the reader begins to question what version of the document is being accessed and the authority of the person who made the changes. That electronic documents can be altered without the author's approval, and without visible signs for the reader, leads to an uncertainty about their integrity. It is possible to encrypt documents so that they are read-only, and to hide electronic watermarks in the text of documents, but hackers can get around these methods and there are costs involved (Zeidberg, 1999).

Longevity

Apart from hazards such as acidic paper, insects, humidity, and vandalism, books and other physical documents have done remarkably well in withstanding the centuries, with the help of librarians and preservationists. Digital media are dependent on technology. Rapid technological change and the mutability of hardware, software, and operating systems, as well as the uncertain life expectancies of the various storage media, cause real concern for the permanence of digital resources.

Traditionally, libraries have preserved the world's print heritage, largely a passive task involving proper storage. Much of the digital content is not owned by libraries but is stored in commercial databases where subscriber licenses generally do not permit libraries to store the data on their own server or migrate the data to other media (Borgman, 2000a). Digital preservation initiatives are working to ensure that electronic journals, Web sites, e-mail messages, learning objects, and other online documents that have long-term value for researchers will be accessible to future generations. MIT Libraries and Hewlett-Packard, for example, have worked together to develop open-source, freely available DSpace technology "to capture, store, index, preserve, and redistribute the intellectual output of a university's research faculty in digital formats" (DSpace Federation, 2003, para. 1).

Personality

Books carry important associations for people, as is borne out by the many private libraries, small and large, ordinary and eclectic. Rarely are books discarded when the reader has finished reading; they are tucked away on a bookshelf, loaned to a friend, or donated to a library. There is even a Web site, http://www.bookcrossing.com, that celebrates the sharing of books as physical objects by encouraging readers to "release into the wild" and track books as they make their way from reader to reader. Electronic documents are easy to toss into the recycle bin or delete altogether. The experience of reading online is generally not conducive to sustained reading, and technology bumps against human factors such as concentration, mood, comfort level, and eyestrain. This is not to say that electronic documents are without personality. One of their most distinctive and exciting traits is their hypertextuality: a single document can contain hyperlinks to other texts and a variety of formats such as audio and video. An e-book permits full-text searching capabilities that overshadow by far what can be learned from a table of contents or an index. Books, in contrast, are characterized by their linearity and are, for the most part, read from cover to cover.

Disintermediation, digital library jargon, the difficulty of conveying a human inquiry to a computer, keeping up with the many changes in online environments, information overload, technostress, and the pressures to be fluent in both print and digital culture can create obstacles to effective digital library use. Irene Sever applied the anthropological concepts of culture shock and ethnocentricity to the experience of "book-oriented library patrons in a 'virtual library' environment" (1994, p. 336). Sever was writing at a time when many library users were not familiar with computers, but although some of the barriers she described have been overcome in large part, such as adjusting to a vertically positioned screen and pressing combinations of keys, much of the spirit of what she wrote holds true for today's digital library users. Sever acknowledged that the process of acculturation is a lengthy one. She saw a role for librarians not just as trainers but as "agents of socialization" (p. 340). What is needed is not learning by rote and repeating routines, but an internalized understanding of digital libraries.

CONCLUSION

Digital technology has reached a point where it is so pervasive that it cannot be ignored. It is a part of society, a part of daily life, and a part of the student and faculty experience in using academic libraries. The digital library enhances the support that a library can offer its university community, particularly in offering convenient, enriched, and enhanced access to library resources and services. This is true in both traditional and distance education environments. At the same time, digital libraries offer access to only a fragment of the world's scholarly documents and they are not easy to use. An understanding of digital library culture can help scholars move beyond grappling with the mechanics of using digital libraries to becoming active contributors. In the next chapter we will consider what it means to interact with digital libraries and electronic information resources as digital scholars.

New Dynamics for Scholarly Communication

Digital libraries and the Internet break down many of the restrictions of space and time to provide students and faculty with unprecedented access to research materials. Computers are not only altering the mechanics and flow of scholarly inquiry but are transforming scholarly communication. Scholars are finding new means to disseminate their ideas and research globally, and traditional relationships among scholars, libraries, universities, and publishers are in a state of flux. Researchers must now have not only the skills to mine the contents of online library databases successfully but also to seek out literature on the Web that may or may not be indexed by search engines, because their colleagues are increasingly discovering alternate means to communicate. This chapter looks at new dynamics and new opportunities in the relationships of users to libraries, in scholarly publication, and in academic culture. We consider in particular how digital technology and electronic publishing are promoting a form of scholarly communication that is based on open access to ideas and research, and the issues this raises for promotion, tenure, and review.

MANY-TO-MANY RELATIONSHIPS IN THE DIGITAL LIBRARY

The traditional library model requires librarians to serve as a bridge between the consumers of information and the providers of information, to select and organize quality information resources, and to be the keepers and the lenders of these resources. The online information environment turns this model on its head. This is not to say that librarians no longer perform these functions, but the one-to-one flow of information has evolved into a model in which library users, publishers, vendors, and librarians are able to interact in "many-to-many" dynamic relationships. As Johnson, Trabelsi, and Tin note, "In the new model, the library serves as a facilitator by offering ongoing support enabling learners to interact and exchange knowledge with others, to communicate directly with the publishers and vendors of information resources, and to participate in a collaborative endeavor to make available rich collections of online scholarly information resources" (2004, p. 350).

The digital library provides an environment in which its users can access and interact directly with a variety of online resources. Many of these resources are evaluated and selected by librarians, and librarians provide ongoing support by developing structured gateways to digital information, troubleshooting access problems, providing instruction and reference services, negotiating online subscription agreements with publishers and vendors, and serving as advocates for their users' information needs.

Users of the digital library are interacting with libraries and with information and knowledge sources in new ways. Faculty may recommend online products that they have heard about from colleagues, seen at conferences, or located themselves. This is not unusual; such recommendations are an extension of the traditional role faculty play in helping to build print collections. What is new is that in recommending online products faculty are making selection suggestions related not only to intellectual content but also to systems, interfaces, and licensing agreements, requiring a much closer collaboration with the library than has occurred in the past. Will a license be obtained only for students registered in a specific course, and what access issues might arise? If the same database is available from different vendors, how does the library balance its preference to negotiate with a known vendor and the faculty member's preference for the interface provided by a different vendor? Students, too, are seeking a voice in recommending online resources for the library's Web site and have come to have high expectations, particularly about access to full-text documents. Faculty and students often demand online products without consideration of the costs of these products, the complex pricing models of some vendors, and affordability in the context of the library's budget.

The online environment facilitates communication between the users of electronic documents and the publishers and distributors of these documents. As Clifford Lynch writes in his survey of the audience, economics, and control of digital libraries, "Publishers and users are talking to each other as never before" (2003a, p. 206). A library delivered via the Web begins to merge with the multitude of resources and services offered through subscriptions as well as freely and commercially through the Web. Online databases frequently include a wide range of services, such as these:

- Help desks that respond to user questions such as how to search and access content.
- Facilities for setting up a personal use area or profile for accessing personal and institutional subscriptions, favorite journals, or saved searches.
- E-mail alerting services for tables of contents, updates, newsletters, and reviews.
- Pay-per-view options to purchase individual articles not available through one's subscriptions.
- Opportunities to participate in online communities and forums.

The library as an entity sometimes gets bypassed altogether as students and faculty access selected links to library-subscribed resources made available through course management systems and institutional Web portals. These methods of access can highlight parts of the library, but at the same time can create a limited view of what is available and even obscure the fact that there is a library at all as the library begins to merge with other educational services and resources.

NEW OPPORTUNITIES FOR SCHOLARLY COMMUNICATION

As scholars contribute to the body of knowledge in a discipline they exchange ideas, theories, and data through peer-reviewed publication and other channels of academic discourse. Gutenberg's perfection of printing and movable type in the mid-15th century advanced scholarly communication dramatically by permitting the dissemination of knowledge quickly and in multiple, identical copies. The Internet has stepped up the pace, permitting a worldwide and almost up-to-the-minute transmission of scholarly ideas and information. Digital documents are fraught with uncertainties pertaining to issues such as preservation, authority, and integrity. These are very real challenges that need to be resolved, but the Internet holds enormous potential for scholars to participate easily in an ever-widening community. Meszaros notes the ability of the Internet to "expand the scholar's world both within and outside the academic community," democratize scholarship, and promote opportunities for collaboration and interdisciplinary exchanges of ideas (2002, p. 36).

Publication in journals remains the gold standard, but scholars are finding avenues for communicating their expertise and research outside the traditional arenas, including contributing to digital repositories, interacting with other scholars online, and developing Web sites. The following initiatives provide a sampling of some of these scholarly contributions to the online information environment.

University of California eScholarship Repository (http://repositories.cdlib.org/escholarship/)

The University of California eScholarship Repository is a part of the California Digital Library eScholarship program to facilitate scholar-driven alternatives in scholarly communication and publication. The repository offers to University of California faculty "a central location for depositing any research or scholarly output deemed appropriate by their participating University of California research unit, center, or department" (n.d., para. 1). It includes working papers, prepublication scholarship, journals, and peer-reviewed series. The repository lists these among its benefits to scholars: an alternative to commercial or self-publishing, quick and efficient dissemination and publication, increased visibility, ability to link to the contributor's home page, statistical tracking to provide usage reports, ability to upload related content such as images and presentations, persistent access, and a sophisticated search mechanism. The process of peer review for journals and series is sped up, and these materials are clearly labeled as peer-reviewed in the repository. The contents of the repository are freely available to all and can be downloaded or e-mailed.

ArXiv.org E-Print Archive (http://arxiv.org/)

ArXiv is Cornell University's e-print service dedicated to making prepublication materials in the fields of physics, mathematics, nonlinear science, computer science, and quantitative biology immediately available to researchers. ArXiv is an automated online distribution system that permits researchers in the sciences to post their research immediately, without having to wait for publication in a journal or for peer review. It is intended as a quick and easy way to communicate research findings and to make this prepublication information freely available to others. ArXiv was founded in 1991, before physics journals were widely available online, and it continues to play a vital role. Paul Ginsparg (2003) reports that there were over 20 million full-text downloads in 2002 and that the access numbers have continued to climb even with the availability of conventional journals online, a phenomenon due largely to the appeal of instant communication and the service's archival function. Other self-archiving services, in which scholars upload their documents to a Web site, include CogPrints (http://cogprints.ecs.soton.ac.uk/) for papers in the cognitive sciences and WoPEc (http://netec.mcc.ac.uk/WoPEc.html) for working papers in economics.

Networked Digital Library of Theses and Dissertations (NDLTD) (http://www.ndltd.org/)

The NDLTD is a public initiative sponsored by the U.S. Department of Education aimed at developing a global digital library of electronic theses and dissertations. The NDLTD focuses on preparing graduate students for digital scholarship and provides them with a highly visible platform for sharing their research. Graduate students have an opportunity to "learn about electronic publishing and digital libraries, applying that knowledge as they engage in their research and build and submit their own ETD [electronic theses and dissertations]" (n.d., para. 4). The collection includes abstracts, and some full text, for theses and dissertations from participating institutions.

H-Net Humanities and Social Sciences Online (http://www.h-net.org/)

H-Net is an international scholarly consortium that provides access to electronic communities in the form of discussion networks dedicated to the exchange of academic ideas, enabling scholars to discuss research interests, share current research, and debate issues with colleagues globally. Scholars edit the "electronic interactive newsletters" or "lists," and subscribers post to these lists by sending e-mail. In addition, H-Net maintains an archive of scholarly reviews published online through the discussion lists and the Web site, providing quick access to timely reviews and permitting interactivity as reviewers, authors, and readers discuss the reviews online.

The OYEZ Project (http://www.oyez.org/oyez/frontpage)

OYEZ was founded in 1989 by Jerry Goldman, a professor of political science at Northwestern University. OYEZ provides access to U.S. Supreme Court audio materials from 1995 and selective coverage for previous years back to 1955. The OYEZ project represents a particularly fine example of a scholar harnessing the potential of the Web to develop a unique digital collection that can be shared with other scholars worldwide.

SHARING IN THE ONLINE COMMUNITY

Not everything on the Internet is available for free, and some resources are very costly, but open-source and open access initiatives are contributing to a digital community that shares intellectual content and educational resources.

Open-Source Licensing

In 2003 the OYEZ project began permitting people to download selections of its Supreme Court audio collection in MP3 versions through a Creative Commons license that permits users to download, share, and create derivative works using the files. In an interview, Goldman explained that OYEZ was doing this to emphasize a positive use of peer-to-peer networking that focuses on sharing rather than withholding information, saying that he envisioned "a community of dedicated listeners and scholars who could add to the audio," particularly by annotating the files and sharing their findings (Lynch, 2003b). Creative Commons is a nonprofit organization founded in 2001 that provides creators of works with an alternative to traditional copyright: they retain copyright of their work but can let those accessing the work know that certain uses are permitted without needing to ask for permission. Licenses are freely available for download from the Creative Commons Web site (http://creativecommons.org/), and a growing number of musicians, photographers, writers, filmmakers, and educators are represented.

Open-source licensing represents a growing trend in academia to forego the often relatively small profits made from educational publications in order to disseminate knowledge to a wider audience. In the spirit of an open university, the authors of the Athabasca University text *Theory and Practice of Online Learning* used a Creative Commons license to make their book available through free download from the Internet, to share freely and widely their knowledge of distance learning alternatives and to encourage scholarly discussion and further development in the field. The editors describe this as a form of "gift culture": "The gift weaves bonds within our community and empowers those who benefit from it to create new knowledge that they can then share with others and with ourselves" (Anderson & Elloumi, 2004, p. xviii). In an unprecedented move to contribute to global knowledge and foster collaboration, the Massachusetts Institute of Technology offers its *MIT OpenCourseWare* resource (http://ocw.mit.edu/index.html), which disseminates freely to the world the high-quality course materials developed by MIT faculty.

Open-source course management systems, such as Moodle (http://moodle.org), Sakai (www.sakaiproject.org), and Athabasca University's Bazaar Online Conference System (http://klaatu.pc.athabascau.ca/), represent a growing trend in helping faculty build course Web pages without having to invest in high-cost course management systems such as Blackboard and WebCT.

Electronic Books

Project Gutenberg (http://gutenberg.net/) provides access to thousands of electronic books on the Internet, primarily literary works in the public domain in the United States. The project dates back to 1971 when Michael Hart, finding himself in possession of a million dollars' worth of computer time at the University of Illinois, decided to enter books and other texts into the computer to permit everyone in the world to have a copy. The project relies heavily on volunteers and focuses not on authoritative editions but on getting high-demand works out to the general public. Other projects that offer electronic books and texts at no cost to the reader include the Online Medieval and Classical Library (http://sunsite.berkeley.edu/OMACL/), available through the Berkeley Digital Library Sun-SITE collections, and the Humanities Text Initiative (http://www.hti.umich.edu/) from the University of Michigan.

Electronic Journals

By the mid-1990s journal publishers, particularly the major publishers of scientific journals, began to move into the online environment. The term *electronic journal* or *e-journal* refers to a number of different entities. The early e-journals were electronic versions of print journals, and this continues to be the case in large part. The main benefit of the electronic versions is accessibility. Many of these e-journals can be accessed through searchable journal databases, although some have their own Web sites. Some e-journals are based on a print counterpart, but they take advantage of digital technology to offer added value not found in the print source, such as extra data, graphics, audio clips, video clips, and interactivity. There has been considerable growth in e-journals that have originated digitally and remain digital only.

Some e-journals are freely available on the Web. *International Review of Research in Open and Distance Learning* (*IRRODL;* http://www.irrodl.org/), is a peer-reviewed e-journal published by Athabasca University dedicated to promoting research, theory, and best practice in open and distance learning. The Association of Historians of Nineteenth-Century Art publishes *Nineteenth-Century Art Worldwide* (*NCAW;* http://19thc-artworldwide.org/), a refereed e-journal dedicated to the study of painting, sculpture, and other fine arts of the period. These and other electronic journals that do not charge readers or their institutions to access them are referred to as *open access* journals. Funding for open access journals often comes from grants and donations. An indication of the growing importance of open access journals can be seen in the Web version of *Ulrich's Periodicals Directory,* the standard source for periodicals information. Ulrich's has added a feature that permits the searcher to limit retrieval to open access, electronic, full-text scholarly journals, many of which are peer-reviewed. A number of providers are dedicated to offering access to free electronic full-text journals, including these:

- BioMed Central (http://www.biomedcentral.com/) is an independent publishing house that publishes open access peer-reviewed research journals in biology and medicine.

- The Directory of Open Access Journals (DOAJ; http://www.doaj.org/) indexes scientific and scholarly research journals in a variety of subjects and languages. DOAJ includes only journals that have peer-review or editorial quality control and provide all contents in full text. The project is hosted by Sweden's Lund University Libraries.

- International Consortium for the Advancement of Academic Publication (ICAAP; http://www.icaap.org/portal/) is a research and development organization devoted to the advancement of electronic scholarly communication that provides free publication services to scholars who are considering developing independent scholarly journals. ICAAP, which is hosted by Athabasca University, also maintains a database of open access resources.

- The Public Library of Science (PloS; http://www.publiclibraryofscience.org/) is a nonprofit organization of scientists and physicians dedicated to making scientific and medical literature freely available. PLoS publishes its own peer-reviewed journals, *PLoS Biology* and *PLoS Medicine.*

The Scholarly Publishing and Academic Resources Coalition (SPARC; http://www.arl.org/sparc/) supports open access publishing. Such initiatives remove barriers to access, increase the visibility of open access journals, and permit rapid and wide dissemination of research in the framework of peer review. Prepublication works, such as the papers in ArXiv, serve an important function in communicating research findings, but peer review remains an important quality-control mechanism in journal publication.

Open access initiatives represent a growing movement to address the rising volume and costs of journal subscriptions, particularly in science, technology, and medicine. Libraries provide access to publications that scholars need for their research, and scholars produce the intellectual contents that are the foundations of library collections. The university system requires faculty to build their academic reputations and to achieve tenure through a publication path that is based on publication in peer-reviewed journals. Pace (2003) describes the catch-22 that academic libraries find themselves in as faculty "assign copyrights of their scholarly endeavors to large publishing houses, who, in turn, sell the content back to college and university libraries at tremendous markups" (p. 24).

Librarians are strong supporters of open access initiatives. Create Change (http://www.createchange.org/), which is sponsored by the Association of Research Libraries, the Association of College & Research Libraries, and SPARC, seek to address what has come to be referred to as "the crisis in scholarly communication." Library budgets are strained by high-priced journal subscriptions and library shelf space is at a premium, with libraries struggling to keep up with the volume of literature being produced. In 1995 Andrew M. Odlyzko described the crisis in terms of the "exponential growth" in the size of scholarly publication, particularly scientific publication, which has tended to double every ten to fifteen years over the last two centuries. Odlyzko notes that growth has slowed in recent years, but that it is still impossible for libraries to keep up with the volume of literature being produced. This volume, along with high subscription costs, is causing libraries not only to subscribe to fewer new titles but also to drop some older subscriptions, a serious concern to scholars who need wide access to the literature in their field.

Create Change (2000, para. 3) has as its main goal "to make scholarly research as accessible as possible to scholars all over the world, to their students, and to others who might derive value from it" and identifies the following strategies:

- Shifting control of scholarly publication away from commercial publishers and back to scholars.

- Influencing scholarly publishers to embrace as their first goal the widest possible dissemination of scholarly information and to abide by pricing policies and practices that are friendly to scholars and libraries.

- Creating alternatives to commercial scholarly publications, both competitive alternative journals in more affordable electronic formats and programs that make scholarly research more directly available to scholars.

- Fostering changes in the faculty peer-review system that will promote greater availability of scholarly research: these changes might include both movement away from *quantity* and toward *quality* as a criterion for tenure and promotion and full acknowledgment of electronic publication as a means of communicating research.

In addition to supporting such initiatives, some libraries are actively developing alternative models for scholarly publication. The University of Arizona Library publishes the *Journal of Insect Science* (http://www.insectscience.org/) at a loss, with future plans to continue offering the publication as an open access journal but to recover costs by charging authors an "affordable" submission fee, which could be considered a research expense (Roel, 2004). The *Journal of Insect Science* accommodates color figures, video and audio clips, and large data sets.

Librarians are also supporting and partnering with not-for-profit publishers that offer licensing, usage policies, and pricing models that are friendly to libraries and their users. JSTOR was developed by the Andrew W. Mellon Foundation to take advantage of information technologies in addressing the challenges libraries face providing access to scholarly journal literature. By converting the complete back runs of participating print journals to electronic format, JSTOR seeks to help libraries cope with storage issues and improve access to the contents of older journal material. JSTOR promotes electronic conversion as a means to handle long-term deterioration of paper copies and through its Electronic-Archiving Initiative seeks "to develop the organizational and technical infrastructure needed to ensure the long-term preservation of and access to electronic scholarly resources" (JSTOR, 2004, para. 1).

Project Muse, a collaboration between the Johns Hopkins University Press and the Milton S. Eisenhower Library at Johns Hopkins University, offers libraries reasonably priced access to the full text of Johns Hopkins UP and other scholarly journals in arts and humanities and the social sciences. Even if a library does not renew its subscription, ownership of the subscribed journals rests with the library. The cost of electronic-only access is less than the print subscription, and Project Muse offers consortial pricing. Increasingly, libraries are turning to consortia of participating libraries and institutions as a means of negotiating favorable pricing for members. Electronic publication, whether it is fee-based or open access, offers hope to libraries for freeing up shelf space and offering a greater volume of core scholarly journals to researchers.

ACADEMIC CULTURE MEETS DIGITAL CULTURE

Publication in an e-journal is faster than traditional publication, speeding up the process by which scholarly information can be shared. Moreover, electronic publication enables scholars to be innovative in their discipline, using digital multimedia to provide access to types and quantities of material that a print publication may not be able to accommodate. Hyperlinking the references of a document can lead readers almost seamlessly to associated documents, where full text is available. Electronic articles can also provide authorship linkages, permitting the reader to contact the author by e-mail, read about the author, or connect to other publications by the author. It is possible to link a document to other documents related to it by subject as well as to reviews. Some electronic articles permit the reader to comment and review, encouraging a dialogue among authors and readers. If the e-journal is an open access journal, this contributes to the empowerment of scholars, libraries, and universities as they take greater control of the flow of scholarly communication and its products. Yet, apart from all of these benefits, faculty who have integrated, or who are beginning to integrate, digital technologies into their research, teaching, and publication have legitimate concerns about the acceptance of digital scholarship in academic culture.

Deborah Lines Andersen (2004) has edited a collection that examines the role of digital scholarship in the promotion, tenure, and review process. She counters assumptions that electronic publication is not as valuable as print publication because it is a simpler and cheaper process, and that the publishers of e-journals do not subscribe to the same academic standards, by considering the ways in which electronic publications are subject to peer review and quality control. The articles in the book indicate that if digital scholarship is to be rewarded appropriately, there is a need to overcome the bias that online is not as good as print and to acknowledge that electronic peer review and editorial quality control are reputable standards. Westney observes that the "candid assessment, evaluation, and institutional recognition of the scholarly use of information technology within the ranks of academe continue to present and remain an unresolved problem" (2004, p. 40).

Not only review committees but also scholars have reservations about electronic publication. It is not surprising that, pressed for time, many academics prefer to pursue publication through the traditional channels rather than risk publication in a source that might not carry the same weight with their peers. Moreover, as much as they may wish to share their research widely, scholars are often bound by the realities of the publishing system. Some publishers consider posting preprints online a form of prepublication and will not accept the work for publication, and authors can find themselves in violation of copyright agreements if they post published work online (Borgman, 2000b). When submitting their work to an online publication scholars need reassurances that the publication is reputable and that their work will be permanently accessible. Kling and McKim (1999, pp. 14–15) discuss scholarly publishing as a "communicative practice" in which scholars "want their reports to be widely read and credited by their target audiences." The authors identify a scholarly work as "effectively published" when it satisfies three criteria that are applicable to both print and electronic publication:

- *Publicity:* The document is announced to scholars so that primary audiences and secondary audiences may learn of its existence. Publicity represents a continuum of activities from subscription, report lists, abstract databases, advertising and special issues, and citation.

- *Trustworthiness:* The document has been vetted through some social processes that assure readers that they can place a high level of trust in the content of the document based on community-specific norms. Trustworthiness is typically marked by peer review, publishing house/journal quality, and sponsorship.

- *Accessibility:* Readers must be able to access the document independent of the author, and in a stable manner, over time. Accessibility is typically assured by institutional stewardship as practiced by libraries, publishing houses, clearinghouses, and is supported by stable identifiers, such as ISBN and ISSN.

Not all disciplines are equally excited about digital technologies. The sciences are much more convinced of the benefits of electronic publication because of a sense of urgency to communicate research and build on one another's findings. Scientists also rely on computers to manage large data sets. Social scientists are digital scholars in their use of computers to store and analyze social sciences data. Humanities scholars are more reluctant to embrace computing because much of their research is based on working with and interpreting physical documents such as diaries, plays, and music scores (Andersen, 2004). This may change as more primary documents are born digital. Speedy publication may be of less importance to humanists, but humanists are beginning to reach wider audiences through open access publication and are exploring the creative potential of digital media.

CONCLUSION

Digital libraries encourage a level of interaction among the creators, distributors, "keepers," and users of information and knowledge sources that is unprecedented. As scholars take advantage of these many-to-many relationships and of the new opportunities to communicate and share their expertise made possible by the electronic environment, they move beyond being digital library users to being contributors and participants, to being digital scholars. It can be anticipated that the reluctance of academe to reward digital scholarship appropriately will dissipate as growing numbers of scholars discover the opportunities of electronic publication, and as peer-reviewed e-journals increasingly appear alongside print publications in the references of research papers and in highly respected indexing and abstracting services. Initiatives such as SPARC and Create Change can help promote an awareness of the validity and benefits of electronic publishing. Those wishing to learn more about the opportunities and issues involved in scholarly electronic publishing on the Internet are encouraged to consult Charles W. Bailey's *Scholarly Electronic Publishing Bibliography* (http://info.lib.uh.edu/sepb/sepb.html). In the next chapter we examine how faculty are using digital libraries in their teaching and course development to meet the needs of distance learners, address different learning styles, and provide flexible approaches to educating adult learners.

CHAPTER

3

Digital Libraries in Teaching and Course Development

With the increasing number of available electronic resources, it is not surprising that teaching and course development have changed. These resources, including e-books, e-journals, full-text journal databases, and the Internet, have found their way into libraries and have become an important source of information for students, faculty, and librarians. In many cases, they are replacing traditional library research tools, such as periodical indexes, and it has now become essential for anyone wanting to become a successful researcher, or to engage in continuing professional development, to be fluent in the use of these tools. This can be a daunting task, even for those who consider themselves to be library literate or information literate. The rate of change in technology is mind-boggling. Database platforms change and vendors introduce new databases and tools on a frequent basis. Librarians are expected to be skilled in the use of these new tools, requiring them to update and upgrade their searching and research skills

33

continually, so that they are able to assist and instruct library users. Faculty must also keep abreast of the changes, both for their own professional development and to allow them to integrate appropriate resources into their courses and guide their students. This chapter will focus on the effect of electronic resources and the digital library on teaching and course development.

THE DIGITAL LIBRARY AND TEACHING IN DISTANCE EDUCATION

Electronic resources and technology have had a significant impact on teaching and course development, both in the traditional university environment and in distance education. Many early distance education classes were largely print-based. In institutions where distance education is the prime mode of course delivery, students will often receive everything they need to complete the course, including textbooks, study guides, student manuals, and other resources. Lists of supplementary material available from the university or college library or local libraries may also be provided for students. Course content and structure are changing as more courses are offered online, with less reliance on paper-based materials. In the transition period between print and online courses, students are sometimes provided with the Web site URLs of useful pages in their printed course materials. Although it can be useful to have this type of information in study guides, it can also be problematic. Because of the dynamic nature of the Web, students may find that the Web site has changed or disappeared. The inclusion of outdated Web resources reflects badly on the course in that the course appears outdated.

With more courses being offered online, it has become possible to integrate e-resources in other ways. Courses now have Web sites, conference boards, chat rooms, and electronic course reserves. These are prime places for the inclusion of electronic resources. Faculty and students can post links to relevant or interesting Web sites, persistent URLs for journal articles, links to research guides and database help sheets created by the library, and any number of other resources that will be useful to learners. In addition, faculty can create assignments for class use that require students to use a prescribed resource or number of resources. For example, at Athabasca University students in ENGL 324 are asked to give an explication of a passage from a Shakespeare play, and are required to pick two terms, and then use the journal database *Literature Online* to discover the context in which the words are used elsewhere in Shakespeare. This assignment not only requires students to use a library resource but also makes it necessary for them to learn how to use a feature of the database other than how to find a journal article, thereby helping to build their information literacy skills.

Increasing students' awareness of the library can be beneficial to their progress in a course. The simplest way to accomplish this is to provide clear links to the library on the course Web site and conference boards. Students on a traditional campus are often not aware of the full range of library resources and services available to them. The absence of physical cues exacerbates the problem for distance learners. Anecdotal evidence suggests that some students finish their entire degrees without knowing that they could ask librarians for assistance, or as is the case at AU, have books mailed to them at no cost. This points to a need for greater promotion of the library to students, faculty, and tutors. We do not suggest that this is solely the role of faculty; indeed, library staff should be attempting to find new ways to promote library services to the entire university or college community. This can be done in a number of ways, including publishing FAQs about the library in staff and student newsletters (for example, see http://www.athabascau.ca/insider/ and http://www.ausu.org/voice/), which increases the library's visibility in the institution and results in greater opportunities for communication with faculty and students. It is common for students in distance education to feel isolated in their studies, as if they must do it all on their own. The promotion of the library and its services to students, through newsletters and other means, provides them with a level of support that they often need. Librarians recognize that searching electronic databases and resources can be overwhelming, and they develop tutorials to help with searching. By posting links on course pages to specific library resources and by pointing them out to students, faculty can help lessen some of the fear that may be created by the prospect of searching.

Students need easily accessible contact information. Contact information for the library, including the e-mail address and fax and telephone numbers, should be provided in several places on the library Web site. It is also important to post library hours on the site so that students know when they are likely to have a library staff member answer the phone. Libraries may also provide Web forms that students can use to request books or journal articles, research assistance, technical assistance, or general information. These forms can be structured to remind students of what type of information the library needs in order to provide the appropriate assistance. For example, a research assistance request form might ask the students to provide their course name and number, assignment number, a list of the sources already consulted, and the best way to contact them. Research guides should also contain links to contact information throughout, in case students require assistance as they navigate through the guides. (For more information on creating research guides, see chapter 7.)

In this new online teaching environment, faculty roles are also changing. Less emphasis is placed on faculty as lecturer. Instead, the faculty member becomes a learning facilitator who leads students into discussions about topics and course content and encourages students to think critically and share their thoughts with others. It is common for professors to require students to post their thoughts about the weekly readings on the class conference board and respond to other students' comments. Activities such as these can, and often do, lead to in-depth discussions of the readings and other related topics, and can include several or all of the students in the class. Several of these discussions may be taking place at once in different threads on the board, and students may post links to articles, Web sites, and other resources. This type of thoughtful, critical inquiry can be promoted in the online conference board environment and result in collegial, scholarly communication between the students and professor.

With the focus on andragogy in the distance education environment, communication between faculty and students has changed. In a teacher-centered classroom the communication structure is top-down: the professor (or librarian) is communicating or transmitting information and knowledge to the student. In a learner-centered environment, communication is tridirectional, providing the opportunity for students to transmit knowledge to librarians or faculty as well, as Figure 3.1 illustrates.

In this model, all three groups are seen as having experiences and knowledge that help the learning community evolve. Because students are usually more self-directed in distance education, librarians and faculty must be prepared to help them further their own educational goals rather than merely transmit a predetermined allotment of information. Such a model allows professors and librarians greater flexibility in the ways that they impart information.

Faculty and librarians need to be aware that students may use electronic resources and the Internet in different ways than academics and professionals do. Their use may be affected by a number of factors, including age, gender, and life experience. As C. Lyn Currie (2000) notes, adult learners often use their life expe-

Figure 3.1. Tridirectional Communication in Learner-Centered Environments

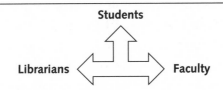

riences as a learning resource. This may affect their use of technology as well. In order to understand better the thinking and work processes of students, it may be advisable to have them "show their work" or describe their research process as a requirement of the assignment. Understanding the ways students use resources will help ensure that relevant learning experiences are provided for them.

In chapter 5 we will examine in detail how students and faculty use digital resources, as well as the concerns that faculty and librarians have about students' use of the Internet in their course assignments. Faculty who ban the use of Web-based sources altogether (Smith Macklin, 2003) risk creating a misconception that Web sites, and by association other electronic resources such as journal databases, never contain quality information. If we teach learners how to identify the characteristics of a scholarly or quality resource, we are providing them with skills that they can use later in life, beyond the hallowed halls (virtual or not) of their postsecondary institution. Indeed, if we prohibit students from using the Internet in assignments we are potentially restricting their learning. Students are often unaware that many library resources are subscription-based. Because of the spread of the Internet and the wide range of freely available materials on the Web, they often believe that library resources are free as well because they are not required to pay to access them. It is extremely important to educate learners about the difference between freely available and subscription resources, so that they become aware of the necessity of evaluating material. Clearly, not all resources that are available on the Web are of poor quality, just as not all material in library databases is scholarly. Evaluating information has always been a research skill, but now it seems to be even more essential because of the sheer quantity of information available to learners. Questions of authority, timeliness, accuracy, relevance, and coverage all need to be considered when reading a source for potential inclusion in a research paper. It is also important to teach learners the difference between a scholarly journal and a popular magazine.

Throughout this book we emphasize the value of digital collections, and of library Web sites as access points. Some truly wonderful and unique collections, artifacts, and documents are now accessible to learners via the Web. Consider, for example, the ease with which access can be gained to the Library of Congress's American Memory project (http://memory.loc.gov) and Library and Archives Canada's digital collections (http://www.collectionscanada.ca). Previously, it was necessary for researchers to visit the physical library, museum, or archives to view certain objects, and although this is certainly still true (and probably will always be) of the majority of special collections in existence, there are many opportunities to save time and research funds by visiting collections online.

By directing their students to library pages as a cure for too much "googling," faculty can reinforce the idea of a library, whether it is virtual or physical, as a gateway to research. Many libraries have compiled lists of sites related to disciplines taught at their institution, and have made them accessible on the library Web site. Resources included here may be chosen by faculty or librarians and should be carefully evaluated before they are added to the list. Annotations may be used to describe the site's focus, to help users determine which ones will be of most use to them. AU Library's Links by Subject (http://library.athabascau.ca/link.php) and the University College Dublin's Subject Portals (http://www.ucd.ie/library/subject_portals/index.html) are examples of annotated resource lists. Other examples of comprehensive Web resource lists are the Open University UK's Routes (http://routes.open.ac.uk/) and Penn State Libraries Online Reference Resources (http://www.libraries.psu.edu/gateway/referenceshelf/). AU Library also provides access to the Digital Reference Centre (DRC; http://library.athabascau.ca/drc.php), a collection of electronic versions of the tools typically found in a traditional reference collection, including dictionaries, encyclopedias, almanacs, and directories. Both the DRC and the Links by Subject pages are regularly updated, and faculty and students are encouraged to recommend links.

COURSE DEVELOPMENT

As technology plays an increasingly important role in higher education, the ways that courses are designed has changed. In distance education and in courses with online components, courses are not developed in isolation by faculty. The course author may be but one person in a team of professionals who assist in the creation of the course. This team may include an editor, a visual designer, a copyright officer, and an instructional media analyst who all help ensure that the course content can be effectively delivered to students through the use of appropriate technologies.

At Athabasca University, the process of course development at the undergraduate level includes seven different phases, and the course author is required to request input from various departments, including the library, in the development process. The library sees the course and suggested lists of materials at Phase 3 of the development process. The library assists course authors in selecting materials in a variety of formats and can provide an overview of the existing collection and what might need to be purchased in order to support the new course. The library's journal database subscriptions offer convenient access to online full-text materials, optimizing the use of materials already licensed for access by the AU community. Librarians are available to support course authors in locating online materials and in linking to this material through the library's electronic course reserves system. Course authors also have access to the *Course Authors Guide* (http://emd. athabascau.ca/resources/ course_authors_guide_jun03.pdf), designed to provide assistance as they work through this process.

It is essential to consider library support for faculty and students when considering the development of a distance education program or course, because the library and librarians are often not only integral in the development of support services for students but also the providers of this support. As technology results in changes in distance education, more librarians are getting involved in course development (Ury, Meldrem, & Johnson, 2000). Often this involvement stems from the perceived need on the part of the faculty member for information literacy or library skills to be built into the course, but it may also extend to having a librarian coauthor and coteach an entire course. At Central Missouri State University, the librarian was coteacher in a nursing course, and focused on teaching the students how to access and successfully use library and Web databases that were appropriate for the course. She interacted with students on the conference board, and via e-mail, often providing the type of assistance they might have received at a reference desk. The subsequent study showed that students found the librarian's presence helpful in their studies, and it also provided ideas for other ways to improve the library's services for distance education students (Dinwiddie & Lillard, 2002).

Librarians can be of assistance to distance education faculty in the development of courses. For example, librarians can help identify resources that meet the needs and requirements of the course and assignments, and assist in the design and development of these assignments so that students have the most opportunities to succeed. They may also create research guides, help sheets for databases and other resources, or other documentation that pertains specifically to the class; they should also promote the available remote access to journal databases and the library catalogue and provide the troubleshooting documentation as well (Rockman, 2004). At AU, students in the nursing and health studies programs access journal database articles through their WebCT learning management system. Because access to databases is sometimes a problem depending on the settings in the Web browser being used, a link to the library's access troubleshooting instructions has been provided in WebCT, as well as in several places on the library Web site.

CHALLENGES IN SUPPORTING STUDENTS AT A DISTANCE

The role of the distance education library in supporting teaching and learning is somewhat different from that of a traditional academic library. It is shaped by the geographical separateness of students and instructors from each other and from the physical library and librarians; as a result, the library's electronic resources may be one of the few collections available to some students, apart from their course materials. Librarians in both traditional and distance environments play an important instructional role. Both types of librarians can provide subject-specific research guides that point out key resources in a subject area, and both teach students how to search the library catalogue and other resources. However, distance education librarians do not have the luxury of receiving visual cues from the student and so are often not able to tell if what they are saying is being understood. In campus-based academic libraries, librarians often provide face-to-face classes to groups of learners, a form of instruction that is usually not possible in distance education. Students in traditional institutions often ask for assistance in finding a book on their topic, and then, once armed with a call number and directions to the appropriate area of the library, will browse through other books on the shelves to find additional resources. This is often not possible in distance education, so librarians must teach users how to find the book in the catalogue, what to look for in the catalogue record to determine if the book is relevant to their topic, how to find other related material, and then how to request the material from the catalogue. Using the library, like much in distance education, is more self-directed and more skills-based than in a traditional setting.

The challenge for distance education librarians and faculty is to find the most appropriate way to teach students the skills they need to be successful when face-to-face meetings are not possible. As we will describe later in chapter 5, library search skills are not always intuitive, and effective online searching requires a broad skill set. One of the library's vital roles is not only to provide learners with the rudimentary skills they need to search the library databases but also to help them reach a level of "searching finesse"—that is, a level of comfort in evaluating the effectiveness of a search and adjusting their search strategies accordingly. Research skills have changed a great deal with the advent of electronic databases and online library catalogues. To be successful in this new electronic environment, learners must be able to construct a Boolean search, recognize that a search strategy that works in a Web search engine (using a plus sign to combine terms, for example) may not be appropriate in a library resource, navigate the various database platforms, and evaluate the information they find. Bibliographic instruction, the instruction provided to learners in the use of library resources, is no longer enough to create successful learners.

Faculty and librarians are working together to discover the most effective ways to teach library and research skills to distance learners, and they often collaborate in developing Web tutorials and guides and in integrating information literacy into coursework. Kelley and Orr's (2003) study of student use of electronic resources found that Web-based tutorials were preferred over for-credit courses, noncredit courses, and instruction via video or handouts. However, we believe that although these Web tutorials can be useful, there are times when nothing can replace direct interaction between the librarian and the learner, whether it be a telephone call or a chat session. Many institutions are exploring the use of chat for reference and instruction, with varying degrees of success, and there are a number of available software packages for libraries wishing to investigate this area, including HumanClick (http://www.humanclick.com/), Live Assistance (http://www.liveassistance.com/), and Live Person (http://www.liveperson.com/). Chat reference allows students to ask questions of a librarian by logging into the library's chat service and typing their question. One advantage of chat reference over e-mail is that there is not the time delay of sending a message and then waiting until a librarian has the chance to read the e-mail and respond. Some software allows the librarian to push pages to the student and cobrowse Web sites with a student. However, many libraries are using commonly available software like AOL's Instant Messenger to provide chat reference. This has the advantages not only of familiarity, because many students use this software on a daily basis, but of cost-effectiveness for libraries. More information about chat reference can be found at Stephen Francoeur's *The Teaching Librarian* page (http://www.teachinglibrarian.org/digref.htm). Bernie Sloan has compiled the *Digital Reference Services* bibliography (http://www.lis.uiuc.edu/~b-sloan/digiref.html). Examples of academic libraries providing chat reference services are Georgetown University Library (http://gulib.lausun.georgetown.edu/resource/chat.htm) and the University of Maryland University College (http://polaris.umuc.edu/library/liveassistance/patronform.html).

Tutorials and help sheets remain important means to reach a wide group of users, and libraries often create, find, and gather these resources and put them in a centrally located page to help make them easily accessible. Examples are the *Finding Information* page at the Berkeley Libraries (http://www.lib.berkeley.edu/Help/finding_information.html), UC Irvine Libraries Online Reference Resources (http://www.lib.uci.edu/online/reference/reference.html), and AU Library's Help Centre (http://library.athabascau.ca/help.php). The Help Centre is available from the main library page, and contains subject- and program-specific research guides created in collaboration with faculty, help sheets for Internet searching, guides to obtaining journal articles from AU Library, library catalogue help, and lists of help pages for citing and referencing and writing. In addition, the library has created database help sheets designed to help users learn how to navigate through various database platforms and conduct appropriate searches in them. Because access to databases and other subscription-based electronic resources is sometimes an issue, the library has created help sheets for users having trouble logging into the library system. Library staff regularly point students in the direction of the help sheets available on the library Web site so that they are aware of their existence if they need help when the library is closed. Feedback from students and faculty on these resources, particularly the research guides and citation guides, has been favorable.

Ultimately, the role of the library in any university or college is shaped in part by the institutional climate. If the library is seen as proactive in providing services and support to members of the academic and student communities, and if faculty and management see the library as being crucial in the success of the institution and its students, the library's role as stakeholder will increase. Unfortunately, there is all too often the misconception in distance education that the university or college library is a last resort for materials, particularly because students often do not live near the home institution. Student access to other university or public libraries is sometimes overestimated. It is the institutional library's primary responsibility to provide materials to registered students and support the curriculum. Consortial agreements at state, provincial, or national levels can certainly enhance student access to collections by offering in-person borrowing privileges at participating libraries.

At AU we are fortunate to be part of two consortia that provide in-person borrowing privileges to students, faculty, and staff. The Alberta Library's (TAL; http://www.thealbertalibrary.ab.ca/) membership includes public, college, and university libraries and provides not only borrowing privileges to users but access to consortial subscriptions to journal databases and other products. The Canadian Universities Reciprocal Borrowing Agreement (CURBA; http://www.coppul. ca/rb/rbindex.html) provides in-person borrowing privileges at participating libraries across Canada. In both cases, students must contact their home library to request that a card be sent to them before they are allowed to borrow materials, and loan privileges vary depending on the institution. Although these programs benefit students, they mostly serve those living in larger centers where the majority of university and college libraries are present and are less helpful in rural areas. Canada is an enormous country, and students located in less populated areas may rely on their local public library, whose mandate does not require it to collect the same types of material available through a university or college library. By promoting an awareness of the resources and services available through the student's university or college library, we are promoting student success.

LEARNING STYLES

In order to meet the needs of learners effectively it is important to consider learning styles. One way this can be done is by including resources in a variety of formats. The use of pedagogically appropriate audio, video, and interactive resources can reach auditory, visual, and kinesthetic learners in ways that other materials may not. Developments in information and communication technologies open up a world of new possibilities. These formats can be worked into learning management systems, electronic course reserve systems, library tutorials, and other course resources. We have already discussed andragogical structures in courses in distance education earlier in this chapter. By including resources geared toward different learning styles we are only enriching this learner-centered environment. In courses where information literacy is being taught, contact between students and librarians should be encouraged by, for example, inviting librarians to participate in asynchronous and synchronous conferencing, integrating assignments into Web-based library tutorials and having the librarians evaluate them and return them directly to students, and providing complete contact information for librarians. The librarian liaison model is popular in some institutions (Sugarman & Demetracopoulos, 2001), in which a designated librarian is the main contact for a particular discipline. A growing number of libraries are offering chat reference services, and this can be another way of providing additional support for students. Due in part to the rapid growth of technology, an increasing number of students enrolled in distance education courses are living in other countries and are of different cultural backgrounds. Obviously, the capability of international students to access electronic resources, and the delivery of physical materials through the postal system, may be affected by their geographical location, and their cultural background can play into the way they approach coursework and their needs as learners.

FACULTY DEVELOPMENT

Many postsecondary classes include assignments designed to help students learn how to use the library and its resources. In order to provide meaningful learning experiences for learners, it is helpful for faculty to be aware of changes in technology as they affect libraries, teaching, and course development, so that their assignments are up-to-date and use resources currently held by the library. There is also increasing pressure from administration and students to use technology in courses (Bennett & Bennett, 2003), not only in distance education but also in campus-based education. Yet, despite this pressure, many faculty are reluctant to implement these changes.

There are several issues at play here. Integrating technology into course structures is seen as requiring a significant amount of time and effort. In addition, many faculty have doubts about the pedagogical benefits of technology, and some tenure-promotion systems do not recognize teaching with technology (Mendels, 1998,

Reich, 1999, Stancill, 1999, and Young, 2002, as cited in Bennett & Bennett, 2003). These are all valid concerns. In our current age of increased workloads and decreased staffing levels, time is something that many people simply do not have. Technology changes at such a rapid pace that it is hard to keep up, let alone have the time to decide whether there are sound pedagogical reasons to implement a particular technology. In addition, tenure and promotion in an institution are still extremely important, as we discussed in chapter 2, and they can have a significant impact on the activities in which faculty participate (Howell, Saba, Lindsay, & Williams, 2004).

The reluctance and indecision about including technology in courses may also be a result of differing comfort levels with technology. Some, the so-called early adopters (Bennett & Bennett, 2003), are comfortable enough and believe strongly enough in the benefits of integrating technology into their courses, even though there may be a perceived lack of institutional support. However, for others who are not as comfortable with technology, the perception of limited institutional support simply builds on their own doubts that integrating technology has enough pedagogical benefits to warrant the time it may take to implement change. In addition, it may be difficult to find the time to develop the needed technology skills, resulting in further reluctance to consider the potential benefits that integrating technology may offer students (Hollar, Sutch, & Nichols, 2001). Clearly, the existence of a course development team made up of instructional media designers and other information technology personnel can be of assistance to faculty and help overcome their reluctance.

Other complaints about using digital resources revolve around the idea of "serendipitous discovery" (Starkweather & Wallin, 1999, p. 655). Faculty members interviewed in Starkweather and Wallin's study often referred to finding something that they did not know existed, or that they wanted, when browsing the shelves of the library. These serendipitous discoveries were a much-desired and anticipated outcome of browsing. It is thought that in an online environment the amount of serendipity in searching is less. Although, admittedly, browsing shelves is difficult (or impossible) in a distance education environment, we believe that serendipitous discoveries are still possible when searching an online library resource. Many journal databases allow learners to browse issues of a journal, and most library catalogues provide users with the opportunity to browse books by call number, which permits a certain amount of serendipity in searching. The number of access points to information are greater in an online research tool because it is possible to search these resources by keyword. No longer is it necessary to know the exact subject heading in order to find material. By entering terms that accurately describe a subject it is quite possible to discover something that the searcher was not previously aware of.

Faculty are very familiar with the culture of higher learning, and the culture of their discipline, but it can be challenging to learn the culture required to use digital libraries effectively. Many libraries offer a variety of faculty training opportunities, including regularly scheduled classes, occasional sessions, and one-on-one meetings between a faculty member and a librarian designed to address the individual's specific needs. Sometimes these individualized sessions are the most successful, because more time can be spent helping faculty members determine exactly what knowledge is required to integrate electronic library resources or other technologies into their courses successfully. Group training sessions vary depending on the institution and the perceived need. For example, the University of Michigan offers a faculty training program called Enriching Scholarship: Integrating Teaching, Information, and Technology, which is a series of workshops and seminars that discuss issues involved in incorporating technology into teaching. Sessions are offered on copyright, information resources, and software. Faculty who have attended sessions before are given the opportunity to present the ways they integrated technology into their courses (Hollar, Sutch, & Nichols, 2001). Institutions sometimes offer annual conferences designed to provide faculty with opportunities to see examples of successfully integrated technology and to learn how to integrate technology themselves. An example is the University of Southern California's annual Teaching and Learning with Technology Conference (http://www.usc.edu/isd/locations/cst/tls/events/tlt2004/). At AU, the annual Learning Services Conference provides a similar opportunity. Designed specifically for AU tutors, the conference helps orient tutors to services offered by different departments at the university. Recent conference sessions have explored AU Library's Digital Reference Centre and the Digital Reading Room. AU's faculty training sessions have varied from teaching participants how to use the electronic course reserves system, to more general sessions identifying the types of services the library offers students and faculty and teaching searching tips in different journal databases. Meldrem, Johnson, and Spradling (2001) note that assistance in the areas of copyright, Web searching, and searching techniques is often appreciated by faculty, and they recommend that librarians be part of the "electronic teaching and learning process" (p. 30).

Ultimately, faculty want to provide the best learning experience possible for their students and therefore need to be aware of the tools available to them that will enable them to do so (Rocklin, 2001). This should be the primary goal of faculty training sessions, and the focus should be on how new technologies can be implemented in teaching and how they will increase student learning. It is recognized that faculty appreciate the chance to try out technologies before implementing them in their courses. Libraries often request a trial of a database before purchasing a subscription to it, and are usually willing to make these trials available to faculty, particularly in the disciplines the database serves. In order for technology, or a specific digital resource, to be successfully implemented, it must be seen as increasing effectiveness or efficiency and must be easy to use, even for the novice. The technology must also be compatible with the individual's goals, values, and philosophy (Bennett & Bennett, 2003). So before attending a faculty training session at the library, it is important to express one's interest in these aspects—most librarians will find a way to make it happen if at all possible!

CONCLUSION

Digital technologies and the specialized needs of distance and online learners are having a significant impact on the way courses are developed and taught. To be successful in reaching students, the focus must be on the learners and on creating a learner-centered environment, where opportunities for students to direct their own learning are provided. The skills needed to locate necessary research materials in this new technological era are complex, so it is essential to consider carefully the resources and services available to students and faculty through their library. Librarians are available to assist students and faculty as they navigate through the library databases and to provide a wide range of assistance in the development of courses. In the next chapter we discuss information literacy, a concept that has far-reaching implications not just for libraries but for teaching and higher education.

Beyond the Mechanics of Online Retrieval: Information Literacy

I n this digital age, the concepts of lifelong learning and information literacy are often discussed in higher education. Administrators, faculty, and librarians are all attempting to find the best way to ensure that graduating students are equipped with the skills they need to be lifelong learners and succeed in a networked world. Many are looking to information literacy as the key.

WHAT IS INFORMATION LITERACY?

What exactly is information literacy? The phrase was coined in 1974 by Paul Zurkowski, and referred to the ability to use information resources at work in order to solve problems (Eisenberg, Lowe, & Spitzer, 2004). The concept was bandied about over the next decade, but it was not until the late 1980s and early 1990s that it came into widespread use. Important works like Patricia Senn Breivik and E. Gordon Gee's *Information Literacy: Revolution in the Library* (1989) and the *Presidential Committee on Information Literacy: Final Report* (American Library

Association, 1989) have influenced the way that librarians and educators think about the topic. The Association of College & Research Libraries (ACRL) released a set of competency standards in 2000, which state that information literacy is the ability to do the following (p. 3):

- Determine the extent of information needed.
- Access the needed information effectively and efficiently.
- Evaluate information and its sources critically.
- Incorporate selected information into one's knowledge base.
- Use information effectively to accomplish a specific purpose.
- Understand the economic, legal, and social issues surrounding the use of information, and access and use information ethically and legally.

Various accreditation organizations have also recognized the importance of information literacy (ACRL, 2003). For example, in their *Characteristics for Excellence in Higher Education: Eligibility Requirements and Standards for Accreditation,* the Middle States Commission on Higher Education (MSCHE) defines information literacy as "an intellectual framework for identifying, finding, understanding, evaluating, and using information. It includes determining the nature and extent of needed information; accessing information effectively and efficiently; evaluating critically information and its sources; incorporating selected information in the learner's knowledge base and value system; using information effectively to accomplish a specific purpose; understanding the economic, legal, and social issues surrounding the use of information and information technology; and observing laws, regulations, and institutional policies related to the access and use of information" (MSCHE, 2002, p. 32).

Clearly, there are similarities in these definitions. The crucial point that both of these documents make is the necessity of knowing what type and how much information is needed, where and how to find it, and how to evaluate and use it ethically for an intended purpose. These standards demonstrate the scope of knowledge needed to be information literate. According to Eisenberg, Lowe, and Spitzer (2004), the exponential growth of technology has resulted in information being more readily available in a variety of formats, including graphs, charts, images, animated graphics, and sound recordings. The number of sources providing information has increased as well. In order to be information literate we need to be able to analyze and understand visual objects, think critically about the information generated by the media, have the computer skills to negotiate and navigate through digital sources, and be able to function in the networked environment that is so prevalent today. Information literacy includes visual literacy, digital literacy, media literacy, network literacy, computer literacy, and basic literacy.

Information literacy is not just a "library issue." It is something that affects teaching and course development, student achievement and completion rates in higher education, and ultimately, the success of university and college graduates in the working world. Making information literacy a part of the institution's mission encourages student success. In environments where it is primarily considered the library's responsibility, information literacy is not tied to the curriculum, and programs provided entirely by the library are often unsuccessful. Context must be considered when designing an information literacy program. For students to understand the importance of information literacy, they must recognize that these skills will benefit them in their studies in their particular discipline. If they do not recognize this, it can be difficult for students to make the cognitive leap necessary to transfer what they have learned about library research and apply it to other areas of their lives.

As the title of this chapter indicates, information literacy goes beyond the mechanics of information retrieval. The ultimate goal of information literacy is creating lifelong learners, because it is recognized that the skills learned can be transferred beyond the walls of academia into the workplace and other aspects of life. In this age of digital information, it is no longer enough to be library literate; one must also be information literate.

It seems that almost everyone is talking about the "information explosion" and the "information age." With the advent and proliferation of the Internet and the World Wide Web, there is much more information freely available to the public. Advances in technology, and the decreasing costs associated with being online, have allowed a mind-boggling number of people *access* to information and the ability to *create* information. Almost every e-mail account seems to come with Web space—a place where you can post your own Web site for free. There are free HTML editors available on the Internet, making it even easier and cheaper for users to create their own sites. WYSIWYG (What You See Is What You Get) editors allow users to create sites without needing to know HTML at all. As a result, the line between information consumer and information producer is becoming blurred

(MSCHE, 2003). Many of today's university students used their first computer in grade school, and they are often more proficient at computing than their teachers or parents. In addition, students are often under the misconception that they can find everything on the Web. Yet the ability to use a computer or surf the Web does not mean that an individual is information literate. Because much scholarly information is now available in electronic format or accessible via online library catalogues, it is essential to be computer literate, but this is only one component of information literacy.

Technology obviously plays a large role in the development of information literacy skills, but it is important to remember that the real focus of information literacy is content—that is, how to find information and evaluate and critically analyze its validity. One must be technologically savvy enough to navigate the Internet and online databases, but this is only one step in the process of becoming information literate.

LIBRARY LITERACY AND BEYOND

The skills needed for research, teaching, and learning have changed significantly over the last few decades. Where common research tools used to include card catalogues; print collections of dictionaries, encyclopedias and handbooks; and periodical indexes in book form, we now see online library catalogues, CD-ROM indexes, full-text online journal databases, and digital reference collections. Many of these changes have occurred because of the rapid-fire expansion of technology. This expansion has resulted in the need to update and upgrade information retrieval skills continually. With fully searchable digital products, the number of access points to material has increased. Instead of simply being able to search by author, title, and subject, it is now possible to search by keyword, ISBN, ISSN, call number, and sometimes, a combination of fields, such as author and journal name, simultaneously. These new access points have resulted in the need to expand what might be considered traditional library research skills. It is essential to be able to create the appropriate search strategy (Boolean searching), choose an appropriate database, and function comfortably with a computer.

Traditionally, academic libraries have offered bibliographic instruction classes to their on-campus students, and in recent years these courses have ranged in topic from learning how to search the library catalogue and the Internet to using specific bibliographic resources, including databases and digital reference tools. In a distance education environment there are fewer opportunities to provide in-person instruction. Librarians must find other ways to reach and teach learners. Where on-campus librarians usually provide information literacy instruction through face-to-face interaction with students, either one-on-one or in a group setting, distance education librarians do not have this luxury, and must therefore encompass all aspects of information literacy in tutorials designed for students who may never come to campus. This presents challenges for librarians. If the goal is to provide active learning experiences for students with different learning styles—experiences that engage them—and that relate to their coursework, it is important to use technologies that provide dynamic interactive learning opportunities while also ensuring pedagogical integrity. In some institutions, librarians may be able to request assistance from the computing services department in designing and programming these learning activities (Behr, 2004), and are therefore not required to learn how to program in Macromedia Flash or some other product. However, at many institutions organizational structure or budgetary concerns make that impossible. If these librarians wish to provide the same interactive opportunities, they must learn how to program in the appropriate language, often resulting in a long delay in the completion of these tutorials. In environments where librarians wish to work collaboratively with information technology personnel on projects, it is essential that they recognize that the cultures are different, and that effective and efficient collaborations are born of open communication and mutual respect. The importance of dynamic learning experiences and information literacy instruction must be recognized at an institutional level, and administrators must be prepared to support these activities financially in order to allow them to occur and succeed. As Behr (2004) notes, the library Web site and services available on it *are* the library for distance students. Therefore, we must be prepared to provide these learners with the same opportunities and services as on-campus students.

Because many library research tools are now available in electronic format only, students must be taught how to construct search strings using Boolean operators, learn about database subject heading structures (which tend to differ depending on the database, and also often differ from Library of Congress subject headings), and understand how to choose appropriate databases. In addition, students are now often faced with material in a greater number of formats. Evaluation of information has always been an important part of instruction in libraries, but given the sheer volume of information available today and the wide variety of formats, even more emphasis must be placed on this topic. It is recognized in the literature that many students, both those in distance education and those in traditional on-campus courses, do the majority of their research on the Internet, so they must be taught not only the best way to search the various search engines but also how to decide whether something is a quality and reputable source. They must be able to separate the wheat from the chaff. These tips might include looking at the endings of URLs. For example, sites with .com as a suffix are often commercial in nature, whereas those ending in .edu or .gov are normally education and government sites. Other evaluation criteria include authority, timeliness, and accuracy. The development of strong critical thinking and evaluation skills not only provides students with greater opportunities for success in school but also prepares them for their professional lives.

Despite the decrease in funding for education from governments, increasing numbers of people are enrolling in colleges and universities. Many of these students do not possess the skills they need to find, evaluate, and use material successfully in their studies (Rockman, 2004). Many students are unable to identify the steps in the research process, including formulating a research question, and are often overwhelmed and perplexed at the thought of researching a topic for a class. With the media promoting the idea that nearly all information is available at the click of a mouse, students have high expectations. For example, some have heard about electronic books and think that all books in the library are available full-text online. Others believe that if they are unable to find the information they need on the first try, the information simply does not exist. To be fair, some students recognize that they need help navigating online information and seek out the assistance of reference librarians. However, many are unaware of the services offered by their library and settle on a hit-and-miss approach to searching for information on the Internet. When they are unsuccessful in finding the material they require, they get frustrated. Yet it is increasingly difficult in this knowledge-based economy to be successful in the business world or to go on to further schooling without information literacy skills.

THE NECESSITY OF EVALUATION

As Breivik and Gee (1989) note, information is not knowledge. Information only becomes knowledge when the person accessing the information knows how to evaluate it and synthesize it. In an ideal world, information becomes knowledge, and knowledge progresses into wisdom. In our increasingly global world, knowledge is power. Unfortunately, it seems that despite, or perhaps because of, the plethora of information sources and available information, knowledge is harder to find. It is easy to be overwhelmed by the sheer volume of information, requiring people to work harder to become knowledgeable about a subject. Developing critical thinking and evaluation skills is a requirement if we want to be able to turn information into knowledge because we must be able to assess the validity and content of information and process it. It is not enough to have information (Wilson, 2001). To help students perform these tasks, we must teach them how to learn, rather than just teach them facts (Breivik & Gee, 1989). Providing active learning opportunities for students is one way to accomplish this.

INTEGRATING INFORMATION LITERACY

Much research has been done on teaching in an online environment. Palloff and Pratt (2003) describe approaches that include creating virtual communities for students enrolled in online classes, designing activities that reach different learning styles, setting out a course structure that identifies clear expectations, and using technology appropriately. Although these considerations are all important for designing an online class that helps students be successful, they also relate to building information literacy into the course's framework. Students in the distance education environment often cannot interact face-to-face with their classmates, the professor, and the university library. By including information literacy assignments that actively involve students, by modeling good information literacy skills, and by engaging students in discussions and encouraging them to think critically about a subject, we can provide students with opportunities to become information literate. Distance learners often must be more independent than their on-campus counterparts, so any efforts to introduce information literacy in the online class setting will ultimately increase the likelihood of success. As much recent research has shown, learning experiences in classes should be active and allow the students the chance to take responsibility for their own learning. It is important to remind students that there is a library, and more importantly, a library staff there to help them with any questions they have about resources. This can help to reduce the sense of isolation that many distance learners feel.

Before the wide accessibility of library catalogues and databases on the Web, distance learners usually relied on librarians to search for materials and send them through the mail. Now that electronic resources are readily available, and the number of students with access to the Internet has increased significantly, students are expected to be much more independent. Therefore, the focus should be on teaching learners how to find the material they need, rather than doing the search for them. As Van Vuren and Henning (2001) note, having a librarian conduct the search and deliver the needed materials allows students to practice skills such as evaluation of materials but does not give them the chance to practice the information gathering skills that are a necessary part of the process.

Information literacy can be integrated into the curriculum in a variety of ways. Some examples follow.

Work with Reference and Instruction Librarians to Develop a Tutorial

Information literacy tutorials can take a variety of forms and can be directed to meet the needs of different users. Here are four superb examples:

TILT (http://tilt.lib.utsystem.edu/)
Created at the University of Texas, TILT is designed to introduce students to research skills and sources through a series of three modules. It is now available for use by other institutions as a result of an open publication license. This tutorial has been developed in two forms, FullTILT, which provides total interactivity, and TILTLite, a version that requires no plug-ins.

MERLIN (http://www.library.umass.edu/merlin/)
Created at the University of Massachusetts Amherst, MERLIN is an introductory tutorial. It is designed to help students identify the steps in the research process and learn how to find and evaluate information.

Bruin Success with Less Stress (http://www.library.ucla.edu/bruinsuccess/)
This tutorial, created by the UCLA Libraries, is designed to teach students about intellectual property, legal issues involved in downloading music, citing and documenting sources, and plagiarism.

CUNY Bilingual Information Competency Tutorial (http://www.hostos.cuny.edu/library/HHCL_New_Web/New_Spanish_Tutorial/revised/tutorialespanol/Index.html)
The City University of New York has created a Spanish-English version of its in-

formation competency tutorial. Containing four modules, the tutorial is intended to help students work through the research process, focusing on library skills and information competence.

Create Assignments That Require Students to Use Specific Library Research Tools

Introducing discipline-specific research tools can be an important way to help students build their information literacy skills. This not only gives students the opportunity to practice their retrieval skills but also shows them where they might find articles and reviews related to the discipline they are studying. By providing students with opportunities to learn what high-quality, scholarly sources look like, we are in essence helping them to discover the range of literature available in the discipline. It is important to remind students that if they are having difficulty accessing or locating material, they can contact the library for assistance.

Require Students to "Show Their Work"

Often students are told they need a certain number of scholarly sources for an assignment, several of which must be journal articles. Requiring students to submit their search strategies and the names of the databases they searched permits the instructor to review the search process. This may make students nervous, so it is important to let them know that the purpose is simply to determine where further instruction is needed.

Collaborate with Librarians on Discipline-Specific Research Guides

Traditionally, libraries have created guides to the literature for specific subjects, often known as "pathfinders." In distance education especially, these guides have morphed to include more than just bibliographies and often include guides to the research process, help with searching, and so on. They may also use streaming audio or video clips as a means of imparting information. Working collaboratively with a librarian on a research guide allows instructors not only to make sure that the appropriate pedagogy is being used but also that their information literacy expectations for students will be met. Once the guide is created and posted online, the instructors can create an assignment that requires students to use it early in the term. This allows them to determine the information literacy skills of their students.

Create a Forum for Students to Post and
Annotate Discipline-Related Resources

The Internet can be a good source for resources, if evaluated carefully. Creating a forum on the class Web site or on the conference board where students can post and annotate discipline-related resources provides them with opportunities to evaluate Web resources and share them with classmates. Students should search for sources, analyze them, and then provide a brief annotation that describes why the tool is useful. This can also be a good way to determine the critical thinking and evaluation skills of the class. An outstanding example of this is the research guide created in conjunction with the graduate-level world history seminar at Georgia State University (http://www.library.gsu.edu/worldhistory/home.htm). Students are involved in the selection and annotation of resources for the guide (Sugarman & Demetracopoulos, 2001).

Invite a Librarian to Participate in the Course Conference Board

It is helpful to invite a liaison librarian or reference librarian from the discipline to participate in the course conference board. The role that the librarian plays in this situation should be fairly flexible, but the librarian should be introduced as someone students can talk to about library services, searching, and information resources. This type of interaction occurred at AU Library when a faculty member in the Master of Distance Education program invited one of the librarians to participate in the conference board for a class to discuss an article about distance library services.

Ask a Librarian to Evaluate or Help Create Assignments
Geared to Information Literacy

When integrating information literacy into courses, it is essential that the assignments reflect current technologies in the library. Instructors may ask a librarian to evaluate the assignment and see if it can be completed with the library's resources. An unfortunate truth is that library databases change regularly. Database platforms are redesigned, and content can change unexpectedly, so it is always useful to verify the status of resources before expecting students to use them.

Request a Course- or Discipline-Specific Resource Web Page

Librarians are continually gathering lists of Web resources available in different subject areas. Instructors may ask a librarian to develop a page devoted to their subject area that includes a variety of resources, such as encyclopedias, dictionaries, and carefully selected Web resources. Then they can post the link on the class conference board and refer to it in class so their students are aware of it.

Collaborate with Librarians on Web-Based Instructional Units

Web-based instructional units on aspects of information retrieval and evaluation that are built directly into courses can be especially beneficial to distance learners, who often do not have the benefit of face-to-face meetings with librarians and faculty. If they work collaboratively with a librarian, instructors not only ensure that information literacy is being taught but also that it is being applied in a way that is relevant to their discipline (MSCHE, 2003). In addition, the librarian may be invited to coteach this unit of the course. This will ensure that both the information literacy skills and the appropriate pedagogy are taught.

Limit Course Reserve Lists

Several things can happen when a course has an extensive reserve or suggested reading list. Either the sources are not used at all or students end up with the notion that the listed books are the only ones they are allowed to use or the only books in the library on the topic. If the number of items on the course reserve list is limited and students are encouraged to seek out their own sources for assignments, they are more likely to take responsibility for their own learning and will be better able to apply it to their own knowledge base.

DEVELOPMENT OF SKILLS

Information literacy is not a skill set that is developed overnight. At lower levels of undergraduate education students should be expected to master the basics: how to formulate research questions, construct appropriate search strategies, discover where to find information and who to ask for assistance, and evaluate information sources. As students progress, they should demonstrate more complex evaluation skills and a greater mastery of information retrieval. Critical thinking is a skill that students gain as they develop, and it is tied to many of the skills involved in information literacy. In addition, information literacy strategies change, depending in part on the discipline the student is studying. It is usually in upper-level courses that students learn about the research methods of the discipline, so it should be expected that the strategies learned in lower-division courses will be modified to suit the specific discipline. For example, evaluation is a key aspect of information literacy, but psychologists evaluate materials differently than historians would. One way to ensure that the information literacy skills being taught to upper-level students are pedagogically appropriate to the discipline is to work collaboratively with a librarian on information literacy instruction. As already noted, in order for an institution to promote information literacy effectively, it must be integrated into the curriculum. Students must feel that it is relevant to their coursework. If the library alone is promoting and teaching information literacy, it tends to be thought of as a library issue and students are more inclined to think of it as relating only to library research. It appears to bear no relevance to the development of research skills in their discipline or to their becoming lifelong learners.

In addition, we must consider *who* we are teaching. Adult learners, for example, tend to be more critical and reflective in their research than younger students (Bontenbal, 2000), but they often do not have the technological skills that younger students have. Therefore, we need to be cognizant of these differences, and tailor our instruction so that the needs of both groups are met. An increasing number of libraries are considering adult learning theory when developing user education programs. As Currie (2000) notes, an adult learner–centered approach allows the librarian to take on the role of collaborator or facilitator when dealing with the student instead of the role of expert, because this approach recognizes that "adult learners enter the library with intentions, memories, and styles of learning" (p. 220).

The needs of different learners can be met in a variety of ways. For example, a Web-based tutorial should be structured in such a way that if an individual learner does not want or need to focus on a particular aspect of the research process he is not required to. Likewise, if an individual discovers that there is an aspect of the process that she wants to spend more time on, or if she wishes to gather further information, the tutorial should be designed to allow her this opportunity. It must be recognized that, particularly with adult learners, there may be a steep learning curve related to technology. Libraries often have tutorials and guides that deal with access problems and database navigation help sheets, and they may also offer basic computer instruction sessions on topics such as how to use e-mail and surf the Internet. In a distance education environment it can be difficult to know exactly what the patron's skills are because there are no visual cues available as there are in a face-to-face transaction. For adult learners who are used to card catalogues and print periodical indexes, the new technological library seems completely foreign and can be very intimidating (Bontenbal, 2000). Common statements from adult learners at AU are that they are "not very computer-literate" and that they are not sure how to search the library catalogue or a journal database.

INTEGRATING INFORMATION LITERACY INTO THE CURRICULUM

If the goal is to integrate information literacy into the curriculum, several things must occur. First, it is essential that the administration, faculty, and librarians understand exactly what information literacy is. Introductory seminars on information literacy should be offered to the campus community. These sessions could be organized or presented by librarians, because they are often the most familiar with the concept, but faculty may want to be involved as well. Second, there must be strong institutional support for information literacy. It cannot be seen just as a library initiative, but as an instrumental part of creating lifelong learners. One way to foster this kind of support is through close collaboration between faculty and librarians. As Curzon (2004) notes, faculty in a variety of positions, including full-time, part-time, and those in academic senate, are all in positions to promote the importance of information literacy. Although it might seem that full-time faculty and those in academic senate have the greatest influence, in fact it is often the part-time faculty members and tutors who are responsible for teaching the introductory undergraduate courses where information literacy will first be introduced. If they are to have this responsibility, their input too must be gathered and used.

Third, once understanding of and support for integrated information literacy have been established, a policy document or standards statement should be created, outlining the role of information literacy in the institution. These statements should reflect the educational goals and mission of the university or college itself. For example, the mission statement at California State University sets out the following goals (California State University, 1985, para. 1):

- To advance and extend knowledge, learning, and culture, especially throughout California
- To provide opportunities for individuals to develop intellectually, personally, and professionally
- To prepare significant numbers of educated, responsible people to contribute to California's schools, economy, culture, and future

All three of these points are reflected in the document entitled *Information Competence at CSU: A Report* (California State University, 1995). The working group that created this report outlined the need to assess students three times: when they enter the university, early in their university careers, and as they graduate, to ensure that they are prepared for their professional and working lives. The overriding goal of the information competence program at CSU is to create graduates who are able to transform information into knowledge and then contribute to the society they live in.

Committees formed to decide what is meant by information literacy at a specific institution should include management, librarians, and faculty members who regularly use the library and its resources in their courses. Once an institution-specific definition exists, decisions about how information literacy will be implemented and the expectations of graduating students can be outlined.

According to MSCHE (2003, p. 5), "Information literacy supports pedagogy focused on the development of effective research, critical thinking, and writing or other communication skills. Most faculty can identify these key characteristics in courses they currently are teaching."

An information literacy initiative, therefore, does not have to start with a radical overhaul of all courses and programs. It can begin by building on the initiatives already being taken by faculty and librarians to increase the critical thinking and research skills of their students. This can lead eventually to the implementation of a more involved information literacy strategy in the institution. A barrier that sometimes prevents information literacy initiatives from moving forward is the perception that implementation will be extremely time-consuming. By allowing the process to begin in small ways, by making slight revisions to existing assignments or putting more emphasis on the development of critical thinking and evaluation skills and the research process, the seeds of information literacy are sown without a significant investment of time. To nourish these efforts, administrators should do what they can to support such information literacy efforts by faculty.

The overall responsibility for the successful implementation of an information literacy program lies with the administration. The administration must believe that integration into the curriculum is the best way to implement the program. But information literacy might be a hard sell to some faculty members who do not see library research as an integral part of their discipline or whose students rarely need to visit the library for resources. As a starting place, administrators should encourage faculty to think about how "information retrieval and evaluation skills are mastered within their areas of instructional responsibility" (Breivik & Gee, 1989, p. 41). Breivik and Gee believe that this will automatically lead faculty to the conclusion that information literacy is the key. Ultimately, students in every discipline need to be able to find and think critically about information. In addition, faculty should be encouraged to engage in professional development activities to strengthen their own information literacy skills and develop strategies for teaching such skills in their courses. Seminars or workshops should be offered, either in a virtual or a physical space. Providing these seminars, encouraging faculty, and responding affirmatively to their efforts—this will help ensure that there is a positive environment where information literacy can flourish.

Some excellent examples of information literacy programs are as follows.

California State University Information Competency Program (http://www.calstate.edu/LS/Aboutinfocomp.shtml)

The California State University system has an extensive information literacy program that includes workshops for faculty and students. In addition to this site that provides information about systemwide initiatives, the Web sites for the libraries of various CSU campuses provide lists of specific resources for information competence.

Information Literacy at Florida International University (http://www.fiu.edu/~library/ili/index.html)

The information literacy program at FIU began in 1998 with a proposal submitted by the undergraduate council to the faculty senate. The program identifies the characteristics of an information literate student, and outlines specific requirements expected of lower-division students. These requirements are linked to various core courses offered at the institution.

University of Louisville Libraries Information Literacy Program (http://www.louisville.edu/infoliteracy/)

This site outlines the mission statement, expected outcomes, and an overview of the program. Also included are tutorials and teaching tips for creating library assignments, and lists of assignments created for various classes. As with the other programs listed here, the focus of this information literacy program is on the need for instruction to be context-based.

University of Massachusetts Amherst Instructional Services (http://www.library.umass.edu/instruction/instructservices.html)

The University of Massachusetts Amherst Instructional Services site outlines its mission statement, provides information literacy tutorials, including MERLIN (http://www.library.umass.edu/merlin/), and subject-specific research guides. The site is divided into sections for students, faculty and teaching assistants, and librarians. Opportunities for evaluation of sessions are provided on both the student and faculty pages.

ASSESSMENT

Finally, assessment is an essential part of any information literacy initiative. As Rockman (2002) notes, libraries want to be able to prove that they play a role in the academic development of students and the fulfillment of the institution's mission. The information gathered during the assessment process, particularly outcomes-based assessment, can support this claim. Outcomes-based assessment can be conducted in several ways. Some institutions use quantitative summative techniques, such as pre- and posttests and questionnaires. This type of data can be useful, but it is equally important that students demonstrate their learned information literacy skills through "academic portfolios (both print and electronic), performance-based assignments and activities, and senior-level capstone experiences and demonstration projects" (p. 192). However, outcomes-based assessment is only one aspect of the process. Although on the larger institution-wide scale, an information competency initiative might focus on all of the key skills needed to be information literate, there should be some attempt at the individual course level to determine the specific needs of those enrolled in the course. Embedded assessment allows an examination of student knowledge and skills and can help determine what has been retained. A preliminary assessment of the students' skills could be conducted through a simple assignment that requires them to use library resources (Rockman, 2002). In 1996, the Indiana University Bloomington Libraries launched their Information Literacy Assessment Plan (http://www.indiana.edu/~libinstr/Information_Literacy/assessment.html). It defines the institution's information literacy goals and builds measurement techniques into the structure of the program.

The following are some techniques for assessing information literacy at the course level.

Library Practicum

In a library practicum, students visit the library during a class session armed with a topic they must research. The instructor and library staff are available to assist students as they attempt to locate information. At the end of the class students submit their search results—that is, their search strategy, journal articles, and other materials.

Journaling or Blogging

Students must keep a journal or *blog*—that is, an online journal—of their course-related information-seeking behaviors throughout the term. They should be encouraged to think critically about the research process and to journal these thoughts.

Annotated Bibliographies

Students create an annotated bibliography of sources they have located on a specific topic. Resources might be restricted to library databases and catalogues, or the Web, or might be a combination of both.

Research Proposals

Using a research proposal as a major assignment in a course can be beneficial in a number of ways. Literature reviews are an essential component of research proposals, so students are required to locate literature related to their topics using library resources and the Internet. Requiring students to submit their literature review or an annotated bibliography of the sources they plan to use in their proposal gives the instructor the opportunity to understand the student's research process and provide additional instruction where needed. In addition, these reviews require students to analyze, evaluate, and synthesize the information they have gathered in order to determine the scope of their projects.

Other Assessment Plans

Assessment plans sometimes originate outside an individual institution. An example is the Washington State Assessment of Information and Technology Literacy (2001), a state-level project designed to assess information and technology literacy at all of the state's four-year public higher education institutions (http://depts.washington.edu/infolitr/). Project SAILS (http://sails.lms.kent.edu/index.php), a collaborative project between Kent State University and the Association of Research Libraries (ARL), is designed to assess information literacy skills development in a standardized way that can be used cross-institutionally. The National Higher Education ICT (Information and Communication Technology) Initiative (http://www.ets.org/ictliteracy) is a joint project between the Educational Testing Service (ETS) and several universities in the United States. The goal of the initiative is to determine through assessment whether students have the skills they need to use digital technologies and function in the information society (ETS, 2004). In addition, both the International Federation of Library Associations and Institutions (IFLA) (http://www.ifla.org/VII/s42/pub/IL-guidelines 2004-e.pdf) and the Association of College & Research Libraries (ACRL) (http://www.ala.org/ala/acrl/acrlissues/acrlinfolit/infolitresources/infolitassess/assessmentissues.htm) have created guidelines for information literacy assessment.

After an information literacy initiative has been implemented, it is also necessary to assess the program as part of the curricular evaluation process (MSCHE, 2003). Just as information literacy instruction includes evaluation, the successes and failures of the program as a whole should also be evaluated and assessed. The assessment process should be considered when the initiative is being developed, and should include prospective time lines for initial and subsequent reviews. These will vary depending on the institution.

As a part of the curricular and program development process, assessment allows the institution to be certain that its learning and teaching outcomes are being met and can help with the justification of expenditures in a particular area. In the case of a new initiative, it is crucial to consider evaluation and assessment during the planning process. There is always a certain amount of unknowns with the first run of a program. Even strategies we think are likely to be a complete success sometimes end up failing, so by building assessment into the process we allow ourselves the chance to fix problems that arise. When developing an assessment plan for an information literacy program, the complete process must be clearly outlined, and any potential barriers to its successful completion should be identified. In addition, decisions must be made about whether the entire student population or just a sample is being assessed and where the responsibility for the assessment lies. It should also be decided what learning outcomes are to be assessed and which criteria will determine success or achievement.

According to MSCHE (2003, p. 39), assessment of an information literacy program should be reflective, integrative, and iterative: "It is reflective in that it supports the practices that faculty . . . already use to improve teaching and learning or to encourage new approaches [and] it provides concrete feedback. . . . It is integrative because of its focus on both institutional and programmatic improvement . . . [and] can help to incorporate the . . . institutional goals for information literacy within the disciplines. . . . It is iterative in that an institution may at any point in this process find it necessary to return to an earlier point and retrace its steps in order to refine the breadth and depth of its self-examination."

If information literacy is integrated into existing courses, we must consider evaluating the program as part of the course revision process. It is a common occurrence for courses to be revised and redesigned in order to maintain their currency, accuracy, and relevance. In the case of integrated information literacy, the course and its information literacy objectives should be assessed before this revision process begins. In courses that require students to use particular databases or a specific technology in order to complete assignments, it becomes crucial to check on the availability and status of the resource. This perhaps should occur more frequently than just during the course revision cycle.

Assessment can be expensive, depending on how it is done. Different units in an institution may have had cause to assess activities in their departments, but they may not all use the same assessment process. The different processes should be evaluated to determine which were successful and which would best allow for appropriately assessing the information literacy program. If an already existing assessment plan is used, the costs and required staff time can be decreased.

CONCLUSION

People who are information literate can translate the skills they have learned into their personal and working lives. Those who have these skills gain the opportunity to be lifelong learners. We live in a knowledge economy, and increasingly the only way to obtain the knowledge we need to be successful in many careers and occupations is by navigating through the overwhelming amount of information available and evaluating it for its relevance. In the next chapter we will consider the skills and knowledge required to search online systems effectively and look at issues involved in the use of digital information in higher education.

Using the Digital Library in Higher Education

D igital libraries offer convenient access to rich collections of scholarly materials, but rarely are they intuitive to use. Cultural barriers
vary, depending on users' experience with computers, and more specifically, their familiarity with libraries and digital libraries. Socialization to
digital library culture takes time. It involves learning the mechanics of
online searching and extends to new interactions with information
sources and with libraries. An understanding of the steps and strategies
involved in online searching is an important precursor to moving beyond novice digital library use to deeper comprehension of the process.
In this chapter we describe the basic steps of the search process and offer
some insights into how to make searches more effective.

We also look at how students and faculty are using digital collections, and at
faculty perceptions of student online information use. This brings us to two
broader issues in digital library research: the ethical use of digital information and
the limits of digital collections. Faculty and librarians have an opportunity to work
together to help students reap the benefits of digital information without
compromising academic standards.

UNDERSTANDING ONLINE SYSTEMS

The skill required to use an online search system varies depending on the type and amount of information sought. For example, a researcher going into a database to learn a few facts or locate some background information does not face the same challenges as a researcher seeking in-depth and varied information on a research topic or performing a comprehensive literature search. The former scenario requires the searcher to select an appropriate database, enter some keywords correctly, and browse the results list for items that appear relevant. The skill set required to complete this task is not undemanding. The searcher must be aware of available databases and select and access an appropriate database for the particular inquiry. Once in the database, the searcher needs a basic familiarity with the search screens, must make judgments about the vocabulary used in the database, and must know how to construct a search statement that a computer program can understand. The searcher must be able to evaluate the results correctly. The task is further complicated when too few or too many items are retrieved, and the searcher is unable to locate the needed information in the result set. This requires the searcher to refine the search using appropriate methods.

For someone working on a more involved research problem the task is even more daunting, given the wide array of databases to search. There may be pressure to formulate queries that will retrieve as much information as possible, but also information that is as relevant as possible. Added to this is the need to ensure that materials that are not available digitally are not neglected in the overall research strategy. The basic steps involved in searching an online database may be outlined as follows:

1. Select the online search system.

2. Access the online search system.

3. Navigate search screens.

4. Formulate the query.

5. Evaluate the search results.

6. Refine the search.

An examination of each of these steps reveals the need for a broad range of skills and knowledge.

Select the Online Search System

In the 1970s, when the online information industry was still taking its first steps, there were only a few hundred databases. In 2004, the *Gale Directory of Online, Portable, and Internet Databases* listed over 15,600 databases and database products developed by more than 4,000 database producers and offered by approximately 3,100 online services and database vendors and distributors (Dialog, 2004). However, most students and faculty have direct access to a fairly limited number of databases, usually no more than the couple of hundred databases available through their library's Web site. This still leaves them with considerable choice. Librarians often create listings of resources by discipline or include this type of information in tutorials to help users select databases.

Searchers will want to take advantage of databases that focus on their discipline, such as *Sociological Abstracts* or *CINAHL (Cumulative Index to Nursing & Allied Literature)*, because this can improve the relevance of a search. Multidisciplinary databases, such as *Expanded Academic ASAP* and *Wilson OmniFile*, are also valuable because of the rich, full-text scholarly content they provide. Most databases limit their full-text offerings primarily to publications from the last 20 years. Older material can be more difficult to locate online. JSTOR, a project of the Andrew W. Mellon Foundation, aims to provide access to a complete back run beginning with the first volume and issue for every participating journal.

Many online products besides journal databases are available to researchers. ISI Web of Knowledge offers Web access to *Science Citation Index, Social Sciences Citation Index,* and *Arts & Humanities Citation Index.* By introducing students to online tools that permit easy tracking of an article's cited references, educators can help students develop a sense of the continuity of the literature in a discipline. Statistical databases, such as *Statistical Universe* from LexisNexis, can be used to encourage students to support their arguments with data. Undergraduate students in particular can benefit from online reference products that offer convenient access to encyclopedias and dictionaries. *Oxford Reference Online* and *xreferplus* offer broad collections of general and subject-specific reference works. It is also important for researchers to be familiar with their library's online catalogue, because these catalogues are increasingly becoming powerful search interfaces that can link searchers not only to records for physical items in their library's collection but to online materials such as electronic journals and electronic books.

Access the Online Search System

Key issues in accessing online information systems and their contents are free versus fee-based, authentication, and licensing agreements. Some of the resources listed on a library's Web pages, such as links to selected Web sites and library catalogues, are free and publicly accessible. The resources that a library makes available on the basis of licensing agreements, such as journal databases, require authentication for remote access. Generally, the library's proxy server prompts a remote user for information such as library bar code or identification number in order to authenticate membership in the library's community covered by the agreement. Sometimes it is necessary to make a few changes in the Web browser configuration in order to be recognized by the library's proxy server. If recognition does not occur, the user may be passed directly to the database log-in screen, which will require log-in information not normally available to the user.

A print-based periodical subscription provides a library with copies of journals that it owns; a subscription to a journal database offers continued access as long as the publisher or vendor is willing and able to make the content available and the library maintains its subscription. Some journal publishers make their content available through their own online journals service; for example, Blackwell provides access through its *Blackwell Synergy* service. Many databases, however, are made available through information aggregators, such as EBSCO and ProQuest. The aggregator is responsible for developing the search system and interface, and it negotiates leases with a variety of publishers for the contents. The aggregator does not own the content, so searchers are sometimes frustrated to find that a journal they previously accessed is no longer available because the publisher has decided to remove it from the aggregator's service. Sometimes there are publisher embargoes on the most recently published issues of a journal in order to protect the publisher from revenue losses resulting from reduced print sales. In some instances the full contents of the journal are not available, and the searcher will find that editorial reviews and so forth are missing. A library's subscription may be limited to a particular collection in the database, and the database may offer pay-per-view options in which the user pays to download articles.

Duplication occurs across online products, with some journal titles appearing in multiple databases. This can actually benefit the searcher because there is then a choice as to which system interface to use to access the title. A library may also subscribe to some electronic journals on an individual basis and not as part of a subscribed bundle. Some of a library's offerings may be available on a trial basis only, giving students and faculty an opportunity to provide feedback. As a library builds its online collections, faculty can play an important role in discussing library and departmental budget allocations and the needs of the curriculum.

Many major databases, such as *PsycINFO* and *MEDLINE,* are abstracting and indexing (A&I) databases that provide citations and summaries about documents, but not the documents themselves. Some databases, such as *Academic Search Premier* and *ABI/Inform,* provide a combination of full-text and A&I based on agreements with the publishers. A searcher who finds only a citation in a particular database could waste a significant amount of time seeing if the full text is available elsewhere. Librarians are working to resolve this by introducing into their Web sites linking software programs that link a searcher from a citation in one database to the full text in another database, or to the record for the journal in the library catalogue.

Navigate Search Screens

The database interface is what the searcher must use to interact with the database program. It is made up of the screens, words, search boxes, pictures, buttons, and menus that display when the searcher enters the database. Many databases offer options to select, such as basic, advanced, publication, and subject search modes, that alter the interface. Some search modes provide only a search box and perhaps some means to limit the search. Others provide screen layouts that allow the searcher to enter terms into a guided grid of search boxes and use pull-down menus to select where the terms should appear in the documents.

Although there is some commonality, searchers are faced with a multiplicity of interfaces as they move from product to product. There are often so many links, menus, and layers that it can be difficult to know the capabilities of the particular database. This makes the help files that databases offer vital sources of information about how to navigate and formulate queries. To avoid being overwhelmed, users may wish to learn how to search one database effectively, gather from it some general principles common to databases, and then move on to learning others.

Formulate the Query

In the process of retrieving information the searcher enters search terms that are matched against the indexed terms in the database. One of the most difficult online search skills to develop is how to take a question posed by a human being and translate it into a string of search terms that a computer will interpret correctly.

The most basic search consists of typing in a few words that describe the inquiry, but results from this sort of search tend to be very imprecise, especially when the database is large. Librarians tend to advocate a step-by-step method to formulating a query (for example, Convey, 1992). The search process usually begins with analysis of the search question so that it can be broken down into its basic concepts. The next step is to translate these concepts into language likely to be used in the database, to think of keywords, subject terms, synonyms, and related terms. Finally, the searcher determines the order in which terms are to be submitted to the database and the relationships among the terms. Exhibit 5.1 outlines this process.

The synonyms and related terms provided in the exhibit represent only a brief listing of the possible search vocabulary. At the point of searching it may be necessary to think of other terms. A search on the two possible search statements suggested here would yield dramatically different results. It may be necessary to drop concepts or add concepts or try variations on the keywords. The sample search statements incorporate a number of search techniques: Boolean logic, phrase searching, nesting, truncation, and proximity operators.

Boolean Logic

The term *Boolean logic* was coined for George Boole (1815–1864), the founder of symbolic logic, a field of mathematical and philosophical study. The Boolean operators AND, OR, NOT can be used to express relationships among concepts and search terms in an online search system. Web search engines vary in their use of Boolean operators. For example, Google supports the use of the OR operator, but Google requires that OR be entered in uppercase, whereas most databases do not distinguish between uppercase and lowercase. In Google, AND is not used because by default Google only returns pages that include all of the search terms, and a minus sign is used to represent NOT. Journal databases are fairly consistent in their use of Boolean operators, although some use AND NOT instead of NOT.

The AND operator requires that all of the search terms be present in the search results; OR requires that any or all of the search terms be present in the results; the NOT operator excludes search results that contain the search terms. A search for *higher learning AND digital technology* retrieves only results containing both terms. A search for *higher learning OR higher education* retrieves items that contain

---

Exhibit 5.1. Steps in Formulating a Search Query

Search question: How is higher learning changing as a result of digital technology?

Concepts:

1. higher learning	2. changing	3. digital technology

Search vocabulary:

higher learning	changing	digital technology
higher education	transforming	ICT
postsecondary education	revolutionizing	computer networks
universities		World Wide Web

Sample search statements:

("higher learning" or "higher education") and "digital technology"

(postsecondary or universities) and (chang* or transform*) and digital W/3 technology

---

either or both terms. If the search specifies *NOT vocational,* the database will exclude from the result set any item containing the word *vocational.* It can help searchers to remember that computers are very literal in their understanding of language. Telling the database *higher education* will not cause it to retrieve synonyms. Telling the database *NOT vocational* will cause it to exclude documents that only mention the word even though they are not about vocational education, causing the searcher to remain unaware of potentially useful items in the database.

Phrase Searching

Quotation marks are commonly used to search for words together and in the specified order as a phrase. In Exhibit 5.1 quotation marks are used to search "digital technology" as a phrase. This strategy should be fairly well-known to searchers given its popularity in Web search engines.

Nesting

The search statements in Exhibit 5.1 use parentheses to nest search terms as a concept, specifying the order in which to process the terms. Computer databases have a built-in order of processing and are unable to make intuitive leaps in order to understand what the searcher wants, but they will process items in parentheses first. A search on ("higher learning" or "higher education") and "digital technology" tells the database to find documents with either or both of the terms in the parentheses and then to take this result set and "AND" it with documents containing the term "digital technology."

Truncation

In Exhibit 5.1 the asterisk is used to retrieve variations on the words changing and transforming. *Chang** retrieves change, changes, changed, and changing. *Transform** retrieves transform, transforms, transforming, transformational, and so on. This saves typing and results in a less cluttered search statement. The addition of a symbol to the ending of a root word to retrieve both singular and plural forms as well as other variations is referred to as *truncation.* The asterisk is the symbol most commonly used for truncation, but different symbols, such as the question mark, may be used in some databases. Truncation is a type of wild card, and some databases also permit a special character to be inserted in the middle of a search term to retrieve words containing any character or no character in the position (*behavio?r* retrieves behavior or behaviour).

Proximity Operators

Proximity operators, such as "with," "near," or "within," allow the searcher to specify the desired location of search terms in relation to one another in a document. The use of *digital W/3 technology* requires that the word *digital* appear in the document within three words of the word *technology.* The notation varies considerably from database to database, so it is necessary to check help files to learn how to use proximity operators correctly.

Additional Search Techniques

Field searching permits the searcher to specify in which field of the record the search term should appear; for example, *ti: digital* tells the database to return only items that contain the word "digital" in the title field. This type of search assumes a basic knowledge of database structure: that the database is a file composed of records and that every record contains segments of information about the document it represents, called "fields," and that each field contains a piece of information about the document, such as title.

Sometimes browsing, rather than entering a search query, can be a more effective way to locate material. Often there is an option to browse by publication, which can be very helpful to a searcher who has a known item in mind or who wishes to see what has been published in a particular journal. There may also be an option to browse by subject, which can help the searcher select an appropriate subject heading under which to search. This is called *controlled vocabulary searching*. Database indexers assign descriptors or preferred terms to the documents, identifying what the documents are about. A subject search retrieves only the documents that have been assigned the term, making it more likely that the document will be relevant.

Most databases provide means to limit a search, usually in the form of check boxes, permitting the user to limit to peer-reviewed publications or full-text documents, or to limit by language, publication date, document type, or other characteristics.

Evaluate the Search Results

Even a well-crafted search statement will retrieve items, often many items, from the database that do not meet the needs of the searcher. The database does not understand the context of a search, it merely checks for occurrences of terms. Some items will be completely unrelated to the search question, some might be peripheral but possibly useful, and others may provide useful information. The searcher will need to browse through the results to determine if the goals of the search were met: the most basic being that as many relevant items as needed have been found in the database and the searcher has avoided calling up a large number of items that are not relevant.

Relevance is connected to two concepts in information science: recall and precision. *Recall* is the ability to locate all the material relevant to a given request. It is not really possible, outside of a lab setting, to determine if all the relevant material has been retrieved, but the searcher aims to retrieve as much relevant material as possible. *Precision* is the ability to locate only the material relevant to a particular search, with the searcher aiming to reduce the number of irrelevant items retrieved. Recall and precision are inversely related: as you attempt to increase one, the other tends to decline, so it is important to strike a balance. If you are too general in your search you will have a high recall, but low precision. If you are too narrow in your search you will have high precision, but low recall (Large, Tedd, & Hartley, 1999).

There are additional criteria in evaluating a search. If the searcher needs the most recent publications on the subject, currency will be an issue. Most academic papers require the use of scholarly or peer-reviewed publications, in which case retrieval of a large number of items from popular magazines and newspapers could be an issue. If the search fails to retrieve a sufficient number of appropriate items, the searcher will need to consider modifying the search.

Knowing how a search system ranks results can help searchers interpret what they find. Sometimes this information is available in the help files offered by the search tool. Some databases put at the top of the results list the items in which the search term appears most frequently. The Google search engine uses PageRank technology, which "interprets a link from Page A to Page B as a vote for Page B by Page A" and determines the importance of a page by the number of votes it receives (Google, 2004, para. 4). As part of the equation, PageRank also takes into consideration the importance of the pages "casting" the votes. The pages with the greatest number of votes from important pages go to the top of the results list.

Refine the Search

If a search retrieves an overwhelming number of items, the searcher will need to narrow the search in order to reduce the number of items being retrieved from the database. This will tend to increase precision and decrease recall. If a search retrieves very few items, the searcher will need to broaden the search in order to increase the number of items being retrieved from the database. This will tend to increase recall and decrease precision. Exhibit 5.2 outlines techniques for narrowing and broadening a search.

Knowing some of the mechanics of online searching and the principles common to most databases can help searchers move toward acculturation to digital libraries. Although few searchers actually proceed quite so methodically, knowledge of this approach can at least help searchers, as one Athabasca University student put it so aptly during a reference consultation, "understand how you librarians think." Some of the necessary skills for effective digital library use are computer literacy skills, including the ability to connect to online systems and print, save, e-mail, and otherwise manage search results. Other skills relate to information literacy, which we covered in detail in chapter 4.

USING DIGITAL INFORMATION IN HIGHER EDUCATION

An incredible breadth and depth of valuable scholarly material is available through digital libraries and the Web. Exhibit 5.3 provides a sampling of some of the unique collections that are being made available to researchers electronically.

Exhibit 5.2. Techniques for Refining Searches

Narrow Search	*Broaden Search*
• Use narrower search terms or controlled vocabulary (subject headings). • Use the AND operator to add a concept set. • Use fewer terms in concept sets (remove ORs). • Use the NOT operator to exclude terms. • Truncate further to the right or do not truncate. • Restrict search terms to specific fields such as title. • Limit by language, publication year, peer-reviewed, and so on.	• Use broader search terms or broader controlled vocabulary. • Remove a concept set, the one least important to the overall search. • Use more synonyms and related terms in concept sets (add ORs). • Remove NOT operators. • Truncate further to the left. • Remove restrictions to fields and limits.

How Are Faculty Using Digital Resources?

A survey of academic institutions across the United States commissioned by the Digital Library Federation and the Council on Library and Information Resources found that 34.7% of faculty indicated they use electronic resources all or most of the time for their research and 61.6% reported that they use electronic resources for research some of the time. For their teaching, 22.7% reported using electronic resources all or most of the time and 69% some of the time (Friedlander, 2002, Tables 17, 20). A survey of faculty at postsecondary institutions in Alabama revealed that only 3.4% of respondents reported that they did not use the Web, 43.5% used the Web to find information, 30.9% found useful information and enhanced it (such as by providing links to related information), and 19.8% used the Web to create content (such as developing Web pages). A recurring theme in the respondents' comments was their ambivalence about the technology: faculty valued the availability of information on the Web but had concerns about the accuracy, reliability, and value of the information. Academic discipline was a factor, with the sciences being more positive about the Web, social sciences less so, and languages and literature the least satisfied (Herring, 2001).

Exhibit 5.3. A Sampling of Digital Collections

Collection	Organization	Contents	URL
Bodleian Library Broadside Ballads	University of Oxford/NFF Specialised Research Collections Initiative	Searchable and browseable data-base of digitized copies of the sheets and ballads held in the Bodleian Library. Includes images and sound files.	http://www.bodley. ox.ac.uk/ballads/ ballads.htm
Digital Morphology	The University of Texas Austin/ National Science Foundation Digital Libraries Initiative	An interactive archive of 2D and 3D visualizations of the internal and external structure of vertebrates and nonvertebrates, using high-resolution X-ray computed tomography.	http://www. digimorph.org/
The Discovery and Early Development of Insulin	University of Toronto/Aventis Pasteur Limited	A collection of over 7,000-page images drawn mainly from the U of T, the Aventis Pasteur Archives, and the personal collection of Dr. Henry Best. Includes notebooks, charts, correspon-dence, published papers, photo-graphs, and clippings.	http://digital.library. utoronto.ca/insulin/
Digital Scriptorium	University of California	An image database of medieval and Renaissance manuscripts from the holdings of a number of U.S. participating libraries.	http://sunsite. berkeley.edu/ scriptorium/

How Are Students Using Digital Resources?

The Internet provides students with remote access to course, library, and other resources and with opportunities to communicate and interact with their professors, classmates, and librarians. At the same time there is a sense of crisis in academia that the Internet is "dumbing down" the quality of work that students are submitting and is increasing plagiarism. In an article titled "How the Web Destroys Student Research Papers," David Rothenberg (1998) laments the effect the Web has had on his students' work, with their bibliographies conspicuously absent of books and their text containing neatly inserted graphs and pictures and unattributed quotations.

The Internet is having a significant impact, but Rothenberg lumps all Web sources and scholarly materials available through library Web sites into the same "don't read, just connect" category. Such a bias is difficult to justify when online availability of peer-reviewed materials from a wide range of disciplines is burgeoning, and libraries are canceling print subscriptions because of shrinking budgets and pressure to provide students with remote full-text access.

An extensive body of literature and research is growing around the topic of student reliance on the Web and electronic information. According to a Pew Internet & American Life Project report (2002), three-quarters of college students said they use the Internet more than the library for information searching. Today's postsecondary students are generally very confident with technology. In 2001, 85% of 18- to 24-year-olds in school or college in the United States used the Internet, compared with 51.5% of those who were not in school (NTIA and the Economics and Statistics Administration, 2002b). Marc Prensky (2001), founder and CEO of Games2 Train, describes a divide between the "digital natives," the kindergarten-to-college set who represent the first generation to grow up with digital technology, and those who have learned to use computers later in life, the "digital immigrants." Digital natives have grown up "on the 'twitch speed' of video games and MTV. They are used to the instantaneity of hypertext, downloaded music, phones in their pockets, a library on their laptops, beamed messages and instant messaging. They've been networked most or all of their lives" (para. 14).

Although they may be able to tear about the Web at lightning speed, it cannot be assumed that digital natives have the research and evaluation skills needed to locate authoritative information appropriate to their academic discipline and use it effectively. Yet there is evidence to suggest that students feel confident about their ability to find and evaluate electronic information. A white paper from the Online

Computer Library Center (2002) on the information habits of college students reported that three out of four students surveyed agree completely that they are successful at finding the information they need for their courses and assignments. Nearly two-thirds strongly feel they know best what information to accept from the Web.

Grimes and Boening (2001) interviewed instructors and students and analyzed Web resources cited in papers in two English composition classes. They found that students were using "unevaluated resources" and that there was a gap between instructor expectations and the resources students were using. The instructors were disappointed with the reliability and quality of the Internet-based research their students cited. Student interviews revealed that the students found it easy to locate sources on the Internet, tended to rely on search engines to locate information, did not seek out librarian assistance, and felt the sources to be appropriate for a college research paper. An analysis of student papers found the following problems with some of the Web sources cited:

- *Authorship.* Authorship could not be determined, author credentials were missing, or credentials were inappropriate for the subject.

- *Currency.* Date of publication or last update could not be determined, or the source was not timely.

- *Recommendations.* There was an absence of awards, reviews, site recommendations.

- *Perspective.* There was some bias, but only one site could be labeled extreme.

- *Audience.* Students were not concerned that a site might be directed to a specific audience or to a specific audience for a specific purpose.

- *Style and tone.* Grammar, spelling, use of formal references, and so on were not a significant problem in the sites, but students were unconcerned with this aspect of evaluation.

- *Quality of content.* An absence of documentation made it difficult to assess quality of sites.

- *Organization of information.* Some sites were poorly organized and home pages were difficult to find.

- *Publisher, source, host.* Some fan sites, personal home pages, even a high school project were included.

- *Stability of information.* Approximately 30% of the sites were unavailable because the student provided an incorrect URL or the site was no longer active.

These are standard evaluation criteria that faculty and librarians need to explain to their students. Students may be confident that they can find appropriate information, but are they really investigating the literature that is important in their discipline? Are they developing the research skills required of tomorrow's scholars? Because many of the documents stumbled on through search engines have not gone through the publication process, or through review and selection by librarians and faculty, students are put in the unprecedented position of being the reviewers and selectors of what constitutes appropriate academic content. Educators and librarians need to help them understand this new responsibility and recognize the continued importance of print materials. It is also helpful to promote the availability of librarian and instructor assistance, as well as the usefulness of library Web sites and other guides to scholarly content on the Web.

Web directories and search tools aimed at academic research can provide students with a useful starting point for Web-based research. Examples include Humbul Humanities Hub (http://www.humbul.ac.uk/), SOSIG (Social Science Information Gateway; http://www.sosig.ac.uk/), and PSIgate (Physical Sciences Information Gateway; http://www.psigate.ac.uk/newsite/). Students often have difficulty distinguishing between resources they are accessing through the library and resources they are accessing through the "free Web." Information about the Invisible Web (see Exhibit 5.4) can get students thinking critically about what search engines can and cannot find.

However, search engines are getting "smarter" and are providing services that increasingly put them in competition with libraries. Google has worked with some of the academic publishers to open up to its indexing what has previously been blocked by subscriptions, passwords, and other search engine barriers. The new product, Google Scholar (http://scholar.google.com/), targets the scholarly literature on the Web, including peer-reviewed papers, preprints, books, and theses. Of course, not everything is available in full text online. Citations and abstracts are provided for subscription-based materials, and searchers are expected to use academic libraries to locate the articles. For books, Google Scholar uses "Library Search" to point searchers to libraries that hold the item and "Web Search" to provide directions to online bookstores. The impact of Google Scholar on academic research, student papers, and libraries is debatable (Sullivan, 2004; Kennedy & Price, 2004). This new generation of search engine will certainly improve awareness of the many valuable resources available through libraries by boldly pushing through the Invisible Web. But how does Google's definition of scholarly compare with a university's definition? What is Google including and not including? What about the special search mechanisms, such as subject searching and limit by publication date, available only when you access and search the subscribed database directly? What about all the full-text content immediately available through library subscriptions? There is a risk that students will use only what they can find quickly and in full text through Google Scholar and skip the visit to the library.

Limits of Digital Collections

Given the huge result sets returned on most searches, the Web seems to lead to an infinite number of information sources. Students are easily misled into thinking that if it is not on the Web it is nonexistent, or at least, not worth bothering about.

The words "limited" and "World Wide Web" may sound like a contradiction, but students who rely exclusively on the Web for research are ignoring an immense print record and are searching a limited collection of resources. Pace observes: "The particular challenge for libraries is to educate users about the walls of digital content that they build up around themselves when deriving content from online vendors, whether access to those resources comes from direct marketing or through library subscription services" (2003, p. 56–57).

Digital libraries can lead to a huge array of scholarly resources, both print and digital, but if students restrict their information discovery to digital resources (and worse, limited collections of digital resources), and ignore the truly vast record of knowledge that libraries have played a role in preserving throughout history, they wall themselves in. In this sense the library "without walls" does have walls. A student who ventures into the library's Web site may select a journal database, limit the search to full text because this is fairly last minute and there is no time to go hunting down articles, and print off a few articles without even venturing past the first screen of results. If the student looks no further, the research paper will then be based on one database producer's collection of journals, only those for which full text has been negotiated, and only the first 20 or so items that are retrieved by the search.

Pace expresses particular concern about the "dot-com vendors." These services, such as Questia (http://www.questia.com/), usually market their services directly to students, offering quick and easy information fixes with tidy packages of 24/7 access to full-text electronic books and journal articles and online features such as citing and quoting tools, personal workspaces, and dictionaries. Students using such services are at least accessing a selected collection of published sources as opposed to the hundreds of thousands of irrelevant and inappropriate Web pages that would be retrieved by a search engine, but they need to be made aware of the limits of a digital collection. Faculty and librarians can work together to encourage students to stretch their information-discovery skills to make use of a variety of databases and online tools as well as accessible print collections.

Ethics of Using Digital Information

In addition to having the skills and knowledge required to locate online information that is relevant and appropriate for the purpose, online searchers need to be aware of the broader issues involved in the use of information sources. Plagiarism is not new, but in an age in which writer's cramp has been replaced by copy and paste, and paper mills are easily accessed through the Web, educators are expressing concern that plagiarism has increased. Based on evidence from a number of studies Scanlon (2003) argues that Internet plagiarism might not be as prevalent as has been suggested, but he also reviews evidence that students have misperceptions about what constitutes plagiarism. He advocates a faculty role in promoting student awareness, focusing on their "educator" role more than their "detective" role (plagiarism detection tools such as http://www.turnitin.com have become quite popular). Scanlon outlines a number of strategies: conduct awareness-raising and institutional self-assessment activities and update policies; be clear about definitions of and sanctions for Internet plagiarism; avoid assigning papers on themes that are too general; work with students to ensure they understand their responsibilities in acknowledging authorship and quoting and citing appropriately; and provide ongoing support to students as they work on drafts of their papers. Web-based guides and tutorials can help promote awareness of plagiarism and how to prevent it. Some particularly fine examples are Acadia University's *You Quote It, You Note It* (http://library.acadiau.ca/guides/plagiarism/) and *Plagiarism & Academic Integrity at Rutgers University* (http://www.scc.rutgers.edu/douglass/sal/plagiarism/intro.html).

When students are familiar with the citation style used in their discipline, they may be more aware of how to manage information sources appropriately. Libraries are an important source for citation manuals, help sheets, online tutorials, and guidance. There are also a number of citation management software packages, such as Reference Manager (http://www.refman.com/), EndNote (http://www.endnote.com/), and ProCite (http://www.procite.com/), that can help researchers manage their sources. Some databases require the searcher to export results to a text file and then import them into the citation management software, whereas others permit the direct export of saved citations into the software. There are databases that support the use of connection files in which the searcher accesses and searches the database without leaving the citation management software, but this generally does not work well for complex searches.

The Internet may make it seem that materials that can be accessed without fees do not belong to anyone, and students pressed for time may take false comfort in believing that if it is on the Internet it can be treated as common knowledge. Understanding the ethical and legal uses of digital information requires much more than an awareness of plagiarism and the need to credit one's sources. The Association of College & Research Libraries identifies the outcomes expected of an information literate student who "understands many of the economic, legal, and social issues surrounding the use of information and accesses and uses information ethically and legally" (2002, para. 1). Such a student is expected to have an understanding of the following issues:

- Privacy and security

- Free versus fee-based access to information

- Censorship and freedom of speech

- Intellectual property, copyright, and fair use of copyrighted material

- Accepted practices for electronic discussion

- Forms of identification for accessing information resources

- Institutional policies on access to information resources

- Preservation of the integrity of information resources, equipment, systems, and facilities

- The legal obtaining, storing, and dissemination of text, data, images, and sounds

- Plagiarism and how to attribute the work of others

- Institutional policies pertaining to the use of human subjects in research

- The use of an appropriate documentation style to cite sources

- The use of permission-granted notices for copyrighted material

A glance at these outcomes can overwhelm. It may be within reach to teach students some basics of "Netiquette" and how to cite sources, and make them aware of institutional policies. Topics such as freedom of speech and fair use are far more complex, and educators themselves may grapple with these issues. Copyright law varies from nation to nation. As the Internet breaks down geographic barriers and promotes unprecedented collaboration at the international level, this can be a point of confusion for colleagues from different countries. For example, U.S. faculty will hear their Canadian colleagues speak of "fair dealing" in relation to copyright, and the legal restrictions are quite different. Faculty are encouraged to consult the copyright offices in their institutions for questions about copyright, particularly when developing online courses. The UT System Crash Course in

Copyright (http://www.utsystem.edu/ogc/intellectualproperty/cprtindx.htm) provides a helpful overview for a U.S. audience and includes a link to a "Crash Course Tutorial" designed specifically for distance learning faculty.

CONCLUSION

Digital libraries provide a timely solution to the needs of a growing group of remote users and distance learners, help libraries respond to rising expectations of information access in the information age, and put valuable digital-only or digitized collections into the hands of researchers. It takes time to learn how to use online systems effectively. Understanding the basic mechanics and issues involved in the online retrieval of information is an important starting point for effective digital library use. The basics include an awareness of some of the various online research products available, a knowledge of how to access online systems and their contents, a familiarity with the interfaces and navigation of a number of databases, a grasp of basic search techniques (Boolean operators, phrase searching, nesting, truncation, and proximity searching), and an understanding of how to evaluate and modify a search as needed.

The use of digital resources in higher learning is expanding among both students and faculty. Instructors and librarians can work together to promote an intellectual climate that will encourage students to look past what can be accessed with a click of the mouse and understand the importance of intellectual honesty in handling information sources. Students need to be made more aware of the continuing importance of the print-based record. Faculty and librarians can work in their institutions to ensure that there is funding to develop and maintain collections of resources that are available in print only, and in the case of distance education, support the delivery of these materials to students. In the next chapter we continue to follow this theme of collaboration in the context of librarians and faculty working together to ensure the digital library supports the needs of a community of online teachers and learners.

Faculty-Librarian Collaboration in Online Teaching and Education

Educational institutions today are in a state of flux. With advances in technology and increasing globalization, administrators and other stakeholders are beginning to see their institutions in different ways. Witness the move to distributed learning and distance education. Institutions of higher learning are now not only serving those who live in their town or city but also students who may never even set foot in the country. The challenges faced by these learners, and by the educators who serve them, are innumerable, but making collaboration an integral part of the institution's service ethic can contribute to the success of a distance education program. As universities and other educational institutions increasingly serve students who are geographically remote from them, libraries face challenges in supporting these students.

The term *distance learners* can mean a variety of things. At dual-mode institutions (those providing courses to students both on and off campus) on-campus students may take one or two distance classes. Providing services to these students is obviously very different from providing services to students who live hundreds of miles away from the institution and are taking all of their courses via distance education, whether it be online or print-based individualized study classes. Students who reside in rural or remote communities may find that access to physical library collections is limited and may be further challenged by dial-up Internet connections. The ACRL *Guidelines for Distance Learning Library Services* state: "Access to adequate library services and resources is essential for the attainment of superior academic skills in postsecondary education, regardless of where students, faculty, and programs are located" (Association of College & Research Libraries, 2004, para. 11). They go on to state: "Traditional on-campus library services themselves cannot be stretched to meet the library needs of distance learning students and faculty who face distinct and different challenges involving library access and information delivery. Special funding arrangements, proactive planning, and promotion are necessary to deliver equivalent library services and to achieve equivalent results in teaching and learning, and generally to maintain quality in distance learning programs" (para. 3).

With the growth in distance education and in digital information, librarians and faculty are forming partnerships to ensure that their students have access to the knowledge sources and academic support they need to succeed in their studies. This chapter will discuss strategies to build collaborative partnerships in the digital library, as well as leadership roles, promotion, and marketing of the library in the institution and the impact that organizational climate and management support have on the development of digital library services.

COLLABORATIVE EFFORTS

In the classroom the professor is primarily responsible for the design and delivery of courses. In a distance education environment, courses are largely the result of the combined efforts of course development teams. At AU, for example, a course usually represents the collaboration of a team that includes a course coordinator, a subject matter expert, an instructional media developer, a visual designer, and an editor. The online educational environment requires an extensive infrastructure to enable the delivery of courses and support services. Distance learning of any type requires the close cooperation of all departments, including instructional or tutorial services, registry, the library, and computing services. Kennedy and

Duffy (2004) talk about the formation of collaborative learning communities, which include all stakeholders, including administrative staff, teaching staff, technical support, librarians, and students. They believe that distance learning initiatives can only be successful when all these stakeholders collaborate. In addition, universities and colleges are being accredited through organizations such as the Middle States Commission on Higher Education, and departments themselves may be subject to review by an accreditation committee in their discipline, further structuring the way institutes of higher learning function.

A digital library, too, can benefit from collaborative and cooperative efforts. In distance education, just as in on-campus education, it is necessary to have a library that is capable of supporting students in all the disciplines taught at the institution. The library also must be able to support the research interests of faculty members. Librarians have always been charged with the task of supporting students and faculty, but they are beginning to rethink their roles in the academic environment. The ongoing changes in education and technology occurring around them have forced this. Rather than being the "keeper of the books" (Cook, 2000, p. 19), they are finding themselves in an increasing number of partnerships with faculty and other departments and they are becoming more proactive. Service in libraries has generally, until recently, been in response to requests from students or faculty. However, as more students search the Internet for information and believe that everything can be found on the Web, libraries are being proactive by promoting and marketing their services and their collections. This is not so much a matter of survival for libraries—although there certainly is a need to justify their existence and expenditures in an age when budgets are ever decreasing—as it is the recognition on the part of librarians that students need to improve their skill in finding quality information and evaluating it. Students must be information literate in order to succeed in this networked world and to contribute to the society and culture in which they live.

Cooperation and collaboration between faculty and librarians is not new, having ranged from faculty requesting library instruction sessions for their classes to requests for guides to the literature and research guides for particular courses or disciplines. The digital library, however, brings new opportunities for collaboration. A review of the literature on faculty-librarian collaboration indicates that much of the collaboration between librarians and faculty relates to information literacy. Although information literacy instruction, whether integrated into the curriculum or delivered through other means such as research guides, does make up a significant portion of the collaboration between the two groups, it is by no means the only collaborative effort in existence in the academic digital library. Collaboration between faculty and librarians has been occurring for many years in collection development, teaching and instruction, assisting with information technology needs, and research. In the digital library these types of collaboration continue, but in slightly different forms.

LEADERSHIP ROLES

Leaders are often seen as single individuals—like the Lone Ranger or Paul Revere—who take charge of the situation and solve problems. But in this current age, collaborative leadership is perhaps more important. It combines this individual power with the thought processes of many individuals. Together we can do many things. Creativity and innovation often occur when people work together. Libraries have been collaborating with each other for years. They provide a good example of what can be accomplished when working together. The day-to-day activity of processing patrons' requests for books from other libraries through the interlibrary loan process is a prime example and living proof that working together is better than working alone (Houbeck, 2002). In addition, libraries have been dealing with the increasing number of electronic resources for longer than most academic departments have, and thus have had to learn how to modify their work flow and use electronic information in the teaching and learning process. This time spent learning the best ways to integrate technology into the higher learning environment has helped librarians emerge as leaders in this area. With the increasing amount of available information, faculty have been pressured to integrate technology into curriculum development and to meet the continually changing needs of learners. Curriculum development has traditionally been the sole domain of faculty, and this pressure is being met with resistance—some quiet, some not so quiet. Librarians are in a position to help faculty meet these new challenges.

COLLECTION DEVELOPMENT

Librarians and faculty have traditionally worked together in collection development to ensure that the library's collection contains not only the most recent material on a given subject but also standard treatises and other important works that are integral to the discipline. The goal in collection development has always been to gather appropriate resources and make them available in a seamless manner (Hufford, 2000). However, in the age of digital information, collection development has changed. Libraries are certainly still collecting these printed materials but they are also collecting electronic resources. Collection of the latter poses a different set of challenges for librarians and educators than collection of printed materials. When building a print-based collection, it is common for librarians to collect items based on a review in a journal or other publication or on the basis of a faculty member suggestion. Some large libraries have approval plans in place, meaning that items come in from a book distributor, and librarians examine them before making a decision about what they wish to purchase. When collecting electronic materials the process is different. As Gandhi notes, "Not many sources review electronic resources" (2003, p. 144). Two that do review electronic resources are Brian Mikesell in the *Journal of Library & Information Services in Distance Education* and Cheryl LaGuardia in *Library Journal*. Librarians usually make a decision to purchase a subscription based on the sales pitch by the vendor, or a trial of the product. Faculty are often invited to try out these products with the library and provide their input before a decision is made about whether to subscribe to them or not. It is also not unusual for vendors to pitch their products directly to faculty. Clearly, in the digital library that supports distance education there is a continued need to obtain the standard printed works in the various disciplines, but electronic materials are essential in the support of distance learners. Although it is always essential to consider an item's intended audience it is perhaps even more necessary when dealing with electronic materials, because some electronic resources are immensely expensive. Consultation with the academic department likely to benefit most from the subscription can help ensure that the product will actually be of benefit to students and faculty and be used sufficiently to justify the expenditure. As libraries everywhere work in tight budgets, more libraries are turning to arrangements for copurchasing discipline-related electronic resources with academic departments in their institution or making consortial purchases through agreements with other libraries.

However, not all electronic collections are costly. As noted in chapter 3, libraries and academic departments frequently collect lists of freely available Web-based resources that are appropriate to specific disciplines taught at their institution and post these on their Web sites. These sources might be Web versions of reference tools including subject dictionaries, encyclopedias, or handbooks, or they may be freely available databases created in specific subjects by other universities, governments, or libraries. These resources are carefully evaluated before being placed on a departmental or library site, and are often annotated. It is common for librarians to request that faculty and students submit sources to them for inclusion on the library's page, and likewise, faculty should feel comfortable requesting that librarians assist with compiling lists of recommended Web resources. Librarians spend a significant portion of their time learning proper searching techniques for various search engines and are aware of how to evaluate sources on the Internet, and the sources they locate can be very useful to both students and faculty.

TEACHING AND INSTRUCTION

In chapter 4 we discussed the integration of information literacy into the curriculum, and specifically into existing courses. The amount of collaboration in these endeavors varies widely, from the librarian providing an instruction session to fully integrated coteaching. As noted earlier, the instructional skills of librarians should be further employed in teaching information literacy to students.

However, in order for these increased opportunities for collaboration to be initiated, two things must happen. First, librarians must challenge themselves to take on even more instructional roles. Academic librarians have always instructed, often at the beginning of a term in a group setting, or one-on-one at the reference desk when papers are coming due, but in this age when there is great emphasis on the necessity of finding, evaluating, and processing relevant information, these instructional roles must come to the forefront. Librarians must remember that they are the experts in information retrieval and be confident in promoting their skills and services. Second, faculty must also realize that librarians are able to assist, by ensuring that their students develop appropriate information retrieval and evaluation skills and benefiting their own research and scholarly activities as well. One of the arguments against integrating information literacy and collaborating with librarians is that it will take too much time, and will draw faculty away from teaching the course curriculum. However, in a collaborative environment where faculty and librarians work together to teach students information literacy skills integrated in the curriculum, faculty can focus on ensuring that the appropriate pedagogy is being used and the curriculum is being taught, while the librarian can teach the necessary information retrieval methods. Ultimately, both need to recognize the other as being experts in their area: librarians in information retrieval, faculty in their discipline. When there is this recognition, the resulting partnership can be extremely fruitful.

The teaching and learning environment has changed, and new partnerships are being formed where they did not exist before. Librarians can contribute to teaching and learning in different ways, including discovering resources that support curriculum development, working to integrate information literacy in the curriculum, fostering a collaborative relationship with faculty, developing online learning resources with faculty, and providing greater access to resources and services (Doskatch, 2003). In addition, distance education librarians often have Web development and other technical expertise, so they can serve as technical advisers and help integrate technology in the instructional design of courses. In courses where there is heavy use of electronic sources, such as electronic course reserves, librarians can also help with copyright and licensing issues and provide access to licensed materials because they are often more familiar with the rules governing the use of licensed electronic resources than are faculty (Gandhi, 2003; Kennedy & Duffy, 2004).

Kennedy and Duffy (2004) note that course design should be collaborative to be effective and efficient. Of course, good communication between faculty and librarians is essential if a collaboration is to succeed (Jeffries, 2000). Relationships and communication between the two groups can be developed in very simple ways. As Sugarman and Demetracopoulos (2001) note, every time a student or faculty member asks a reference question and when bibliographic instruction takes place, mini-relationships are formed between the librarian and the faculty member or the student. The basis for these relationships is the immediate information need, but it does start the communication process. Because responding to reference requests and providing instruction are two main components of an academic reference librarian's job, librarians and faculty are initiating these relationships on a daily basis. Acknowledging that we are working toward a common goal—to build the critical thinking and information literacy skills of students—is the best foundation for collaboration (Cook, 2000). Faculty will find librarians very receptive to collaborative projects, because librarians recognize that these activities not only increase the visibility of the library in the institution but also help establish the importance of the library in educational endeavors (Sugarman & Demetracopoulos, 2001).

MARKETING THE LIBRARY AND ITS SERVICES

Just a few years ago it was thought that libraries as we know them would disappear and be replaced by virtual or digital libraries. Librarians would not be employable, because everything would be available on the Internet and everyone would automatically know how to find what they needed (Nims, 1999). We now know that this is unlikely ever to happen. But academic libraries, both those serving on-campus and distance students, are changing. Today, fiscal realities in education are forcing the library to promote and market its services to a greater extent, and to a wider audience. Although it is recognized that libraries remain an essential part of any institution of higher learning, and integral to the success of students, libraries regularly face decreasing budgets for collections, staff, and technological infrastructure and resources. To add to this fiscal difficulty, the costs of both print and electronic resources are increasing, resulting in some rather large headaches for library directors as they try to figure out the best way to make sure their collections meet the current needs of the programs being offered while staying in their budget.

Libraries in recent years have also seen a decrease in the number of students and faculty who use their facilities (Kelley & Orr, 2003), in part because of the popularity of the Internet. Distance education libraries have the added problem of being invisible to remote students unless the students are aware of the library Web site. Many distance learners believe that because they do not attend classes on campus, there must not actually be a campus to go to, nor a physical library. At Athabasca University the only time we see students in significant numbers on campus is at convocation in June. The library often provides tours to the graduating students, and the number of students who have been surprised that there is a physical library with real books is astonishing. Clearly, there is a need to educate our students about the library and discover ways to increase its visibility in the institution. In on-campus libraries it is common for students to hesitate before coming to the reference desk to ask a question for fear of looking stupid. In distance education it is possible for the librarian to speak to students regularly on course conference boards (if they have been invited to participate by faculty), and this provides an opportunity for students to ask their questions of the librarian without fear, while also building in an opportunity for them to learn about the library's services (Lillard, Wilson, & Baird, 2004). Being able to contact a librarian by e-mail and telephone can be similarly liberating for students.

Comfort with technology is another issue that librarians and faculty face. Distance education has long been considered the realm of adult learners returning to school. Although this is changing, the thought of searching for the materials they need in the online environment can be daunting for older students who did not grow up with computers. This may also be true of some faculty, especially faculty who began their careers with print-based research tools. Librarians are aware of the need to provide professional development opportunities to faculty. These interactions help faculty make better use of the library's resources and also provide the library with an opportunity to win over faculty who are dubious about the digital library. Faculty who are informed about the library's services are better positioned to ensure that their students use the library effectively as a key resource in their education. Literature in distance education has shown that the seamless integration of online library services in the course structure actually helps with registration and retention of students (Gaide, 2004).

Libraries may be marketed in a variety of ways. They often produce documents that outline their services and new activities or resources that are held in the library (Jeffries, 2000). These documents may be published on the library Web site or in staff and student newsletters on a regular basis. Links can be set up from the library catalogue to show users the newly acquired library materials, and a "what's new" section on the Web site can feature news about updates to the Web site, new journal databases, or other resources. It is also important that library staff make themselves visible by presenting at departmental meetings, workshops, and conferences to promote awareness of changes occurring in the library. Another form of marketing is branding—that is, producing bookmarks, pencils, book bags, and so forth with the library name emblazoned on them. Many libraries send electronic notices about services to students and faculty as well.

These are examples of "librarian-only" marketing, but collaborative marketing and promotion can be even more effective. How does collaborative marketing take place? Faculty-librarian collaboration on research guides and the integration of information literacy into the curriculum can be a starting place. For example, as the guide is being created, the faculty member can forward the in-process document to colleagues in the discipline and request their input. Once the guide is completed, the authors can copresent it to the faculty member's colleagues at the next departmental meeting. Heller-Ross (1996) believes that the institution's administration should encourage faculty to invite librarians to departmental meetings. This not only promotes the library and its services but also helps keep the department informed about useful resources. Adams and Cassner (2001) concur, suggesting that faculty invite the liaison librarian to attend departmental meetings to discuss the needs of the department. This can also help establish lines of communication between faculty and librarians, something that is essential if librarians are going to be successful in assisting faculty in research, teaching, and locating resources. In an educational environment where students regularly use the Internet to research their papers it is essential to make faculty aware of library services, because it is recognized that faculty are usually the first line of contact with students and can have tremendous influence on their perception of the library (Adams & Cassner, 2001).

An examination of the literature proves that collaboration is seen as an important issue in higher education today. At the 2003 American Library Association–Canadian Library Association joint conference in Toronto, several presentations were given on collaboration, and speakers included not only librarians but also faculty. Joint faculty-librarian presentations at conferences on the integration of information literacy and other collaborative efforts not only serve as professional development but also promote the role of collaboration and the library's role in the institution.

THE IMPORTANCE OF ORGANIZATIONAL CLIMATE

Organizational climate plays an enormous role both in the development of the digital library and in collaborative efforts. Administrative support for the library, based on the recognition of its importance to the success of students and faculty, is crucial if the library is to be able to support adequately the institution's programs and research areas. In the digital world, growth in the library means more than just adding to the collection, or potentially finding a new physical space in which to house collections. It can also mean acquiring new technological infrastructure, and making a bigger financial contribution to support the growth of digital collections. Administration must also acknowledge that it is the institution's responsibility to provide the necessary resources for students to be successful, and that services for off-campus students should be equal to those services available to on-campus students. If the organizational climate or the fiscal reality is such that this is not the case, it can be difficult and frustrating for library staff attempting to support users in their research endeavors. In addition to providing fiscal support for the library, it is also important that the administration support collaborative ventures between faculty and librarians to integrate information literacy and develop curriculum.

However, as essential as collaboration is in this digital and distributed age, our organizations are often not set up to support or facilitate it (Wilson, 2000). Therefore, we must find ways to bring about small changes that allow collaboration to occur more easily. Ideally, the management or administration of the institution will recognize the importance of collaborative efforts and attempt to build a sense of collegiality in the workplace that fosters collaboration.

CONCLUSION

Faculty-librarian collaborations benefit everyone. Students in particular benefit because they not only learn about their discipline but also how to find the sources needed to research it. When collaboration is successful, the agendas of both the faculty and the librarian are fulfilled (Cawthorne, 2003). As Cook (2000) notes, "A teaching library is a proactive library with a multitude of connections to the rest of the academic community" (p. 22). Budget, technical limitations, and workload all have an effect on the integration of library services in distance education, as well as on collaboration (Heller-Ross, 1996). The next two chapters provide case studies of collaborative information literacy projects at AU and an electronic course reserves system that was developed in-house.

Collaborating on Information Literacy: Case Study 1

Athabasca University Library actively promotes information literacy. Our information literacy efforts range from creating subject-specific research guides and tutorials in collaboration with teaching faculty to cowriting an information retrieval course with a faculty member and creating a number of other tools in-house. These resources were designed to help students become better users of digital materials and increase their confidence in their own information retrieval and research skills by providing them with the foundation they need to navigate the digital world successfully. This chapter will describe some of these projects.

RESEARCH GUIDES

At Athabasca University, librarians and faculty collaborate on projects designed to provide better support to students, and faculty consult with librarians about the availability of resources, course development, and even the best way to direct students to materials. This open relationship has allowed librarians and faculty to work together in creating subject-specific research guides that provide students with searching assistance and tips on how to evaluate materials and cite sources properly. The library has created several such guides, and this is an ongoing activity. Research guides are initiated either by faculty or by librarians, and are created using examples taken directly from courses or sample topics that are relevant to the discipline, so that students will find the guides pertinent to their studies at AU. Because AU serves a distance student population, these guides are quite detailed, covering all aspects of the research process. We recognize that many of our students are reentering schooling after time away and many are unfamiliar with the best ways to obtain the materials they need for assignments. Their difficulties stem sometimes from a lack of knowledge about searching electronic resources, and sometimes from the misconception that there is not a library available to help them. A large number of our students are not enrolled in programs with us, but in single courses to help them fulfill the graduation requirements of their home institutions. They often fail to realize that they have access to books and electronic materials through AU Library. The *Report on Student Usage and Satisfaction with Athabasca University Library Services, 2004* identified a need to promote awareness of library resources and services and to improve navigability of the library Web site, which are ongoing projects (Athabasca University, 2004). Clearly, the need to reach these students is great. AU Library hours are 8:30 to 5:00 p.m. Mountain Time, Monday to Friday, so we recognize that there are many times when students may need assistance but are unable to ask us directly. Online help and research guides, although not a substitute for talking to a librarian, are detailed enough that they cover some of the most frequently asked questions and help students think about their research topics in a different way. In addition, contact information for the library is provided throughout each guide, and is regularly presented to students on other library Web pages to remind them that there are real people available to answer questions or provide further assistance should they need it.

Although guides are tailored to specific disciplines, the overall format for all the guides is similar. Each is divided into several sections, including "Getting Ready to Search," "Searching," "Evaluating," and "Writing and Citing." These are deemed the most important topics in doing research. Our goal is to help students begin thinking about the entire research process, from formulating a research question or in-

Exhibit 7.1. Psychology Research Guide: Getting Ready to Search

Athabasca University 🔺

Getting Ready to Search

Getting Ready to Search   Searching   Evaluating   Writing   Citing

A) Understand the assignment

B) Think critically about your topic

C) Develop a search strategy

A) Understand the assignment

The most important part of this whole exercise is understanding what you need to know and where to find that information. Without that understanding, it would be like trying to find your way through a forest blindfolded.

terpreting assignments, to finding the information they need, to evaluating information sources. In the "getting ready" section, we identify some important issues for students to think about, including thinking critically about the topic, considering deadlines, and putting a search strategy together. (See Exhibit 7.1.) As we have already noted, many students do not have the skills they need to be successful in coursework. These students find searching databases and catalogues overwhelming and frustrating because they have not learned how to construct a Boolean search and have not developed their critical thinking skills. In discussing the various steps involved in the preliminary stages of research we are teaching students how to begin their research, and providing them with a tool they can come back to as they continue their studies.

"Searching," the second section of the guide, contains information about how to search useful tools, such as the library catalogue, selected journal databases, and the World Wide Web. (See Exhibit 7.2.) This section describes the types of material to be found in each resource, and we also provide screen shots from the library catalogue and journal databases so students can see a visual representation of the steps involved. We believe this to be beneficial, because it helps reach individuals with different learning styles. Among the hardest things to teach students is that

Exhibit 7.2. Psychology Research Guide: Searching

Athabasca University

Journal Databases, continued

Getting Ready to Search   Searching   Evaluating   Writing   Citing

When researching a topic in Psychology, many different databases can be used. We have chosen five that can provide useful material for research in this subject area. Please be aware that each of these databases have strengths and weaknesses and that it is always **essential** to evaluate the information you find. It is recommended that you search several databases for information as not all databases index the same journals.

PsycINFO

PsycINFO, is considered by many psychologists to be the most important psychology database in existence because of its wide range of coverage and the types of documents it indexes. These include dissertations, journal articles, book chapters, and conference proceedings. AU Library will interlibrary loan articles and book chapters if we do not have copies of them in our print or electronic collections. For more information on the Interlibrary Loan process click here. In its original form was a print periodical index. While it has made the transition to electronic format, it is still a citation database - it only provides access to the citation and abstract for articles.

PsycARTICLES

PsycARTICLES provides full text articles from 42 journals published by the American Psychological Association and other related organizations. Journals indexed in this database are also included in PsycINFO.

there are different ways to search and that the same strategy is not necessarily best for all types of resources. It is essential to encourage students to think creatively about their topics and to be prepared to formulate different search strategies depending on the resource being searched.

As noted earlier, evaluation is a key part of the research process. Each guide focuses on key points to consider when evaluating sources, including accuracy, currency, timeliness, and authority. When dealing with Internet sources, evaluation becomes even more important because of the sheer volume of information available. By asking students to think about these aspects of evaluation, we are helping them develop the critical thinking skills they need to be successful in their education and in their professional lives.

Once students have found the necessary information and evaluated it, they must begin the writing process. The writing section of the guide contains tips and lists of writing guides. Guides that deal with specific types of writing related to the discipline are especially useful. The final section contains information on citing resources in the style appropriate to the discipline, and provides a list of resources, available either on the Web or in the library's print collection. In addition, a link to the university's plagiarism policy is included. This section of the guide is crucial because students often demonstrate difficulties citing sources appropriately.

The collaborative process in these guides varies depending in part on the faculty member's schedule. It can be difficult to find time to meet with faculty, especially because many of our faculty members are based in other locations. Some faculty members are very hands-on in the process and want to be involved in every aspect of the guide, whereas others are less directly involved. In addition, from a library standpoint, finding the time to work on a guide is difficult, particularly because the number of students contacting the library for assistance is ever increasing.

During the creation of the psychology guide (http://library.athabascau.ca/ help/psyc/introduction.htm), the librarian and faculty member were able to meet several times to plan out the guide's overall framework and to decide which types of resources should be included. After these initial meetings, both parties set aside an entire day to write the guide and tailor it specifically to psychology. The majority of the guide was actually written on that day, after which the librarian finished up the remaining sections and reformatted the guide from MS Word to HTML using Macromedia Dreamweaver. Once the HTML pages were finished, the librarian posted the guide on a temporary site for editing and revisions before posting it on the library's Web site. An assistant in the psychology department was responsible for editing the guide and brought the suggested changes to the librarian. The librarian received additional input from other faculty in the Centre for Psychology, and subsequent revisions were undertaken. The collaborative process was very informative. The librarian, who at the time had only been with the university a short time, found herself challenged to think about the way that she imparted information to students in psychology, and learned about some of the assignments and requirements of the discipline. Likewise, the faculty member gained a more complete understanding of the types of student support services the library provides. The faculty member also kept the librarian on track in the amount of "library jargon" she used, and ensured that the goals of the academic discipline were met in the guide.

Guides intended for use by graduate students have a somewhat different feel. Where in an undergraduate guide the focus is on the research process itself, in a graduate guide the focus shifts to the types of resources available. In the guide for the Master of Arts Integrated Studies (MAIS) program (http://library.athabascau.ca/ help/mais/main.htm), the librarian worked with the director of the program in the development process. (See Exhibit 7.3.) It became clear almost immediately that, because of the program's multidisciplinary nature and the level of studies being undertaken, the focus of the guide would be different. Rather than emphasizing the steps involved in research, there was a definite shift toward the resources available to help students find the materials they need.

It is assumed that students in graduate-level programs have already developed basic research skills in their undergraduate work. The MAIS program is multidisciplinary, which often means that students must search a wider range of databases to find information than they would in a single discipline. Because of the differing platforms on which databases are available, and in order to ensure that we met student needs, we included help sheets for a larger number of databases. These instructions extend beyond the simple searching tips provided in an undergraduate guide, explaining how to sign up for table of contents alerts with specific journals. The director also asked that instructions on how to search databases that incorporate popular media sources, such as newspapers and magazines, be included, because often his students need to consider popular or alternate perspectives on a subject in addition to scholarly sources. Finally, a section about archival and library collections available on the Web was included. The amount of scholarly material on the World Wide Web is increasing significantly, and the inclusion of these

Exhibit 7.3. MAIS Research Guide: Introduction

Athabasca University

MAIS Research Guide

A collaborative project between The Center for Integrated Studies and AU Library

The Research Process   Library Catalogues   Journal Databases   Digital Reference Centre

Digital Reading Room   Internet Searching   Libraries & Archives   Home

If you can only see the Athabasca University logo above, click here.

This guide is designed to help you become a better researcher. It identifies important elements in the research process, and key resources available through AU Library's Information Gateway (library catalogues, journal databases and other online resources) and on the Internet. It has been prepared jointly by the Centre for Integrated Studies and AU Library and is intended for the use of students enrolled in MAIS courses.

If, at any point you have questions or concerns about this guide please feel free to contact AU Library or the Centre for Integrated Studies. We'll be happy to help!

sources was considered an essential part of the guide to promote student awareness of the many valuable scholarly digital collections available electronically. (See Exhibit 7.4.)

HELP CENTRE

The Help Centre (http://library.athabascau.ca/help.php) houses the library's information literacy tools, including the research guides, a help sheet for finding journal articles through the library, and a tutorial on searching the library catalogue. We have tried to make our Web site and tools as useful and user-friendly as possible. The Help Centre provides extra support in some of the important aspects of research, including citing sources in the style appropriate to the discipline; searching the Internet, journal databases, and the library catalogue; and engaging in various types of academic writing. The Help Centre is designed as a sort of "self-help" place: somewhere students go when they need assistance in a variety of areas, but do not wish to contact the library directly. The Help Centre comprises resources created in collaboration with faculty, resources created by other AU departments, and carefully selected instructional tools and tutorials from other institutions.

Exhibit 7.4. MAIS Research Guide: Library and Archival Collections

Libraries and Archives

Most libraries and archives have online catalogues that are freely accessible to everyone. AU Library has a selected list of library catalogues from Canadian libraries on our website under Use Other Libraries.

We also subscribe to a database called WorldCat that provides acess to over 40 million catalogue records from libraries in Canada, the US and selected international countries.

Recently, an increasing number of libraries and archives are digitizing parts of their collections and making them accessible on the web. Below is a selected list of resources that may be helpful to you as you pursue your studies.

Inventory of Canadian Digital Initiatives

This list of Canadian Digital Initiatives has been compiled by the National Library of Canada. It includes resources in French and English. Many of the sites are from government organizations, universities or libraries.

The Canadian Poetry Archive

This archive, created by the National Library of Canada, includes poems and biographical sketches of English and French Canadian poets.

The Canadian Heritage Information Network

This site is an extraordinary collection of information and images about Canadian Heritage. Also included are guidelines for those interested in creating and managing digital content.

ArchiviaNet

THE DIGITAL REFERENCE CENTRE

AU Library provides access to a Digital Reference Centre (DRC) (http://library.athabascau.ca/drc.php), a collection of digital reference tools including dictionaries, encyclopedias, almanacs, atlases and maps, directories, and data and statistical sources. The DRC contains both items that are freely available on the Web and subscription-based products, such as the *Oxford English Dictionary Online* and *Encyclopedia Britannica*. Distance learners, especially those living in remote or rural areas, frequently do not have physical access to the reference collections generally found in an academic library. Reference books play an important part in the research process, permitting students to gather background information and basic facts and locate the terminology used in relation to a subject. For students unfamiliar with the functions of the various tools, descriptions and annotations are provided for each category. Each resource type is described at the top of the category page to help students decide whether the sources found on that page are likely to be of assistance to them.

INFS 200: ACCESSING INFORMATION

We have seen that faculty and librarians can work together in a number of ways to ensure that students have the necessary skills to find their way as scholars in an increasingly complex information landscape. As one AU academic who has worked closely with librarians to promote student research skills expressed it, "A perception of advantage easily leads to enthusiasm, to the sense of joint endeavor that is the best part of partnerships" (Mouat, 2003, para. 6). This same academic, a historian, was assigned the task of developing an introductory level course called INFS 200: Accessing Information, in collaboration with an AU librarian.

With the rapid expansion of the online environment throughout the 1990s, the need to teach AU students the skills to deal with the information explosion became increasingly apparent. The course, developed as a print-based course in 1995–96, quickly became dated as "Veronica," "Jughead," and "Gopher" gave way to the World Wide Web. In 2003–04 it became time once again to recognize "mutual advantage," and the academic, needing a major course revision, approached one of the authors of this book, who was looking for a way to promote effective use of the library's online resources. The two agreed that this version of INFS 200 would need to be online in order to keep up with the dynamic nature of the course content. Material that they agreed did not need to be online are provided to students in print form, to avoid off-loading printing costs onto the student.

The librarian was responsible for writing the first three units of the course, which provide opportunities to learn about how knowledge is organized, techniques for searching and retrieving information from online systems, and the application of online search strategies to finding information on the World Wide Web. Skills related to the research process and to thinking critically are emphasized. In the final unit, the academic provides a historical and sociological perspective that examines issues involved in the "information revolution" and the impact of technological change. The course makes use of the multimedia opportunities available in an online environment, using animations to demonstrate online searching and Web hypertext to link to the library's online resources and external sites. Images, video clips, audio clips, and other digital resources enrich the material. The two authors agreed to cotutor the course, and students are encouraged to use e-mail as their primary mode of interaction with the tutors and to submit their assignments electronically. (See Exhibit 7.5.)

Exhibit 7.5. INFS 200: Accessing Information

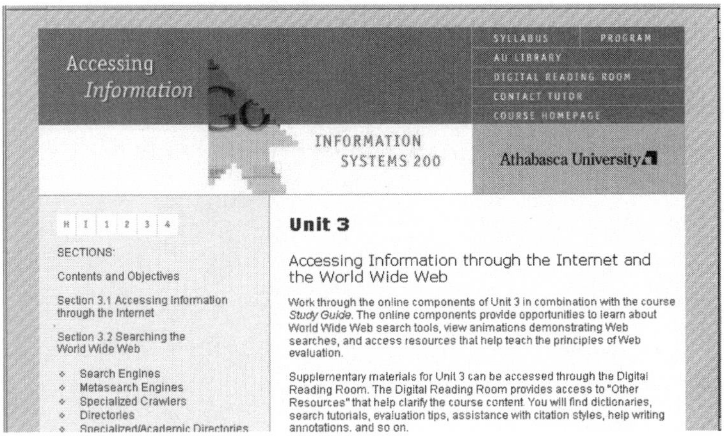

CONCLUSION

Information literacy can be promoted to students through a variety of strategies. The collaborative development of discipline-specific research guides and courses on information retrieval are but two ways. Essential in the development process is a strong recognition of the skills that each person brings to the creation of these resources. Equally important is the discovery of a common goal—in most cases, the success of students and their development as critical thinking, information- and knowledge-savvy individuals. In the next chapter we discuss the collaborative process in developing an electronic course reserves database, the Digital Reading Room.

Collaborating on the DRR and Reusing Learning Resources: Case Study 2

The DRR, or Digital Reading Room (http://library.athabascau.ca/ drr/), is an enhanced electronic course reserves system developed in-house at Athabasca University. This chapter provides an overview of the DRR, its collaborative development and use at AU, and its relationship to a growing trend in education: the sharing and reuse of online learning resources.

THE DIGITAL READING ROOM

In a traditional higher education environment, on-campus students access course-related materials placed "on reserve" by their professors by visiting the course reserves desk in the library. In some cases the course reserve material is required reading, and sometimes it is recommended as an enhancement to the course content. Generally, students face short loan periods, high fines for late returns, and limited copies. By the mid-1990s a number of university and college libraries in the United States began to convert their paper-based course reserves systems to electronic reserves (Association of Research Libraries, 1996), and a growing number of libraries now offer remote access to course reserves.

In a distance learning environment, the handling of paper-based course reserves is more complex for the library because the materials need to be delivered to the student, usually through the postal system. Loan periods cannot be short because they have to accommodate the delivery and return of the materials, and multiple copies of materials such as videos, kits, and books are required. Some distance libraries, such as AU Library, dispense with late fines altogether. AU uses a number of models to accommodate delivery of required and supplementary course materials to students:

- Bundled required readings may be included in the course package that is sent when a student registers in a course.

- Study materials may indicate that there are required materials that students need to request from the library in order to complete the course requirements successfully.

- Study materials may include listings of supplementary materials that students can optionally request from the library.

Many of the required and supplementary materials that students request from the library are journal articles. The library maintains a master file of articles placed on reserve. When students call, e-mail, or fax to request these materials, library staff photocopy them and process the packages for delivery through the university's mailroom.

By 1999 the library sought a digital solution to course reserves that would take advantage of advances in information and communication technologies and the increasing availability of full-text journal content in the library's databases. After some experimentation with the reserves module in the Innovative Interfaces Inc. library system, AU Library decided in 2002 to develop its own enhanced electronic reserves system, the Digital Reading Room.

The DRR does not entirely replace the print-based model, but it permits online delivery of materials already available in electronic form. Faculty have the option of submitting digitized versions of print-based readings, but such an approach is costly and time-consuming because copyright in Canada is far more restrictive than the fair use of U.S. copyright law. To avoid copyright infringement under fair dealing, Canadians must get permission from the copyright holder before scanning and mounting copyrighted materials online. The preferred method of providing online access to material in the DRR is to create persistent, durable links to articles available through the library's database subscriptions and to link to material available on the "free Web." Access to material that is not available digitally is provided through Web forms that streamline the process of requesting materials from the library.

The DRR offers a number of benefits to students and faculty:

- Students have immediate access anywhere and anytime to digital resources.
- Students are provided with a convenient method for requesting nondigital resources.
- Access to materials selected by course authors provides students with examples of quality online resources, and promotes awareness of the rich scholarly content available through the library's databases.
- Course authors can address a variety of learning styles by including a range of formats, such as hypertext, video clips, audio clips, and interactive Web sites.

Every course in the DRR has a digital reading file in which materials are divided into required readings and supplementary materials, and further divided into units, lessons, or weeks that correspond with the study schedule in the course. Course authors are encouraged to include a brief annotation for each resource, and there are areas to add course descriptions, notes and instructions, and links to library, course, program, and other resource pages. Students access course materials through the "Student View," and course developers use the "Admin View" to create and update the files. Exhibits 8.1 and 8.2 show both of these views of a digital reading file for the AU course INFS 200.

The Digital Reading Room has been designed as a multidisciplinary knowledge database and is in this respect quite different from many other electronic course reserves systems that restrict access to students registered in a particular course. The DRR permits a student in communication studies needing research materials that could possibly intersect with other courses, such as marketing, to search across all of the files in the DRR and retrieve materials that match the entered search terms. Anyone in the world can access the Digital Reading Room and most of its digital reading files. However, a DRR user must log in as a member of the community served by AU to access materials made available through the library's licensing agreements, and must log in as a student registered in a particular course to access copyright-cleared digitized resources.

Exhibit 8.1. INFS 200 Digital Reading File: Student View

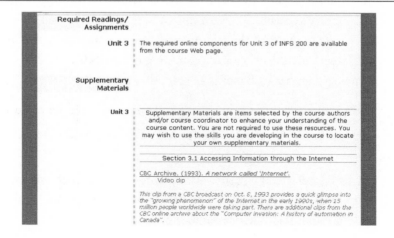

Exhibit 8.2. INFS 200 Digital Reading File: Admin View

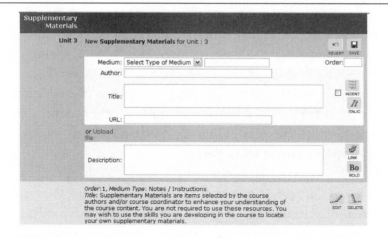

THE COLLABORATION

The library initiated development of the DRR, but the project grew in partnership with the university's Educational Media Development (EMD) unit, which coordinates the course development process at AU and provides the administrative, technical, and creative services for designing and developing courses. In the developmental phases of the Digital Reading Room, EMD provided expertise in instructional technology and visual design, working with the electronic resources librarian to develop the system in-house using open-source software, including MYSQL database management software and PHP scripting language. EMD continues to play a key role in informing course authors and course coordinators about use of the DRR in the development of new courses and in course revisions.

The DRR project evolved as the university moved to take advantage of expanding online infrastructures to improve the flexibility of learning systems for students by using "appropriate e-learning pedagogy," digital systems, and digital resources (Athabasca University, 2002, p. 11). From the beginning, the university's teaching faculty provided much of the inspiration for the development of the DRR. With the introduction of a new graduate-level program in integrated studies, the program director came to the library seeking ways to facilitate the delivery of high-quality resources to his students and encourage interdisciplinary access to resources among students and faculty. Other faculty were looking for ways to update listings of supplementary materials and improve their knowledge of the online resources available through the library.

The electronic resources librarian guided the project in a manner that was responsive to the expressed needs of faculty, including tools to format bibliographic citations properly, a broken link checker, a statistical tracking mechanism, and training and assistance in using the library's digital resources. There was some initial concern about protecting intellectual property in such an open system, and the library needed to promote awareness of the DRR as a means to facilitate access to and sharing of learning resources. If they choose to do so, faculty can password-protect materials, such as papers or presentations, that they wish to make available only to students in a particular course. There was also concern about workload, but the use of the services of the Digital Media Technology unit for data entry has done much to resolve this issue. An issue that has been far more difficult to contend with is the instability of database content. Because database aggregators lease journal content rather than own it, they and their customers are at the mercy of publishers who decide to pull their journals from a database. Aggregators are working to improve their warning system so that libraries can prepare for cuts and make other arrangements to provide access to the content. The situation is less serious when the lost material is supplementary and faculty can substitute alternate readings, but it is very disruptive in the case of required readings in which curriculum is tied to database content.

THE EVALUATION

The DRR was developed as a multidisciplinary research database that students can use not only for their course materials but for further resource discovery; however, it could be expected that use would be tied in large part to the extent to which a course requires students to use the DRR or promotes the DRR as a source of supplementary resources. The *Report on Student Usage and Satisfaction with Athabasca University Library Services* revealed that only 13% of the random sample of 300 undergraduates and 15% of the 373 graduate students surveyed used the DRR (Athabasca University, Institutional Studies, 2004). The Master of Arts Integrated Studies students indicated a higher usage at 54%, which is not surprising given the program's considerable overall use of the DRR. Student suggestions for improving the DRR included adding more materials, providing more instruction, and making the system more "user-friendly." Students who had not used the DRR identified lack of awareness as the key factor that would need to be remedied to encourage student use. Of the graduate students who used the DRR, 89% reported that it was either very useful or useful in meeting their information needs. Of the 10 undergraduates who responded to the question about satisfaction, 7 found it very useful, 2 found it useful, and 1 found it not useful at all.

An additional evaluation that specifically targeted DRR effectiveness and surveyed students registered in courses for which a digital reading file had been implemented confirmed lack of awareness of the DRR as a key issue (Gismondi, Johnson, Ross, & Tin, 2005). The random sample of 39 undergraduate students and 11 graduate students found that even though the students were taking courses for which a DRR had been created, only 32% said they had accessed the DRR. Of those who had not accessed it, 52% indicated that "they didn't know that a DRR existed." When asked if they would access the DRR in future, comments from non-users indicated that many would do so if they could download materials to print, if the materials helped them meet the course learning objectives, and if materials were current and well-organized. Most students who used the DRR said that what they liked best about it was easy access to materials.

Both the student usage and satisfaction survey and the DRR evaluation used telephone interviews and reproduced student comments verbatim. The student comments provide a valuable snapshot of human-computer interaction and inform future development of the system, particularly when it comes to promotion, instruction, contents, and ease of use. The DRR evaluation also surveyed a sample of faculty who had used the DRR in course development. Eight of the 10 faculty surveyed indicated that they would implement a DRR in future courses, and comments included praise for library support in developing digital reading files and easy access to online materials. A clear indication of the survey was that faculty want more training opportunities for themselves and improved DRR support and instruction for their students.

BEYOND COURSE RESERVES: REUSABLE DIGITAL RESOURCES

The development of the DRR as an enhanced electronic course reserves system and searchable multidisciplinary database of learning resources coincided with Athabasca University's foray into learning objects and digital repositories. The DRR not only permits users to search across learning resources listed for different courses and programs but also includes a function for conveniently reusing resources from other digital reading files. The developer of a digital reading file can run a search across all of the files in the DRR and select from the results appropriate items to add to the course under development.

The DRR promotes a conception of learning resources as reusable entities, commonly referred to as *learning objects.* The use of learning objects in technology-supported learning has become increasingly popular over the last decade or so. Although they can certainly be used to enhance classroom instruction, much of the impetus behind the funding for learning object initiatives comes from pressures to develop course materials that meet growing demand for e-learning and lifelong learning. The sharing and reuse of learning objects nationally and internationally is seen as a cost-effective way to meet the needs of e-learning programs (Littlejohn, 2003). The Learning Technology Standards Committee (LTSC) of the Institute of Electrical and Electronics Engineers (IEEE) has worked to create and promote standards for making instructional technologies interoperable and learning objects internationally shareable. There is some debate about what constitutes a learning object and whether the definition should include nondigital resources. David Wiley defines a learning object as "any digital resource that can be reused to support learning" (2000, p. 7).

The main purpose of learning objects is to provide instructors with educational resources that can be reused and reassembled to support particular instructional goals. The term *granularity* refers to the size of a learning object. A learning object can be as small as an image, an interactive map, or an electronic article, and as large as a course unit or even an entire course. Imagine you are developing or teaching an introductory art history course and you want to find creative ways to convey key concepts to your students. You could incorporate a variety of learning objects from many different sources: interactive animations to teach line, color, shape, and so on; a virtual tour of a major art museum to demonstrate how the art of the past reaches the public today; and an interactive time line to introduce the chronology of the major periods and figures to be studied in the course. The learning object is put into context by the instructor and used in a way that fills a pedagogical purpose, and the student adds meaning as well. Take, for example, Marcel Duchamp's altered image of the Mona Lisa (the one with the moustache and goatee). It is a powerful image, bound to elicit a reaction, but how might it be used to meet different pedagogical ends in an art history lesson, a sociology lesson, or a philosophy lesson?

Learning object repositories provide for a structured approach to the access, discovery, sharing, and reuse of online or digitized materials in curriculum development. A particularly fine example of a repository of online learning materials can be found in the Multimedia Educational Resource for Learning and Online Teaching (MERLOT; http://www.merlot.org/). A consortium of higher education institutions offers MERLOT as a means for faculty to enrich their courses. MERLOT is a searchable catalogue of peer-reviewed, annotated, reusable educational materials organized by discipline. Membership is free and provides opportunities to contribute materials, comment on resources, create assignments explaining how particular material can be used in a course, create a personal collection of resources, and become a peer reviewer. Other initiatives to provide structured access to reusable online educational materials include Campus Alberta Repository of Educational Objects (CAREO; http://www.careo.org/), the University of Wisconsin System Institute for Global Studies database (http://www.uw-igs.org/), and the Wisconsin Online Resource Center (http://www.wisc-online.com/).

ADLIB (http://adlib.athabascau.ca/) represents Athabasca University's contribution to the development of learning object repositories. The project has been developed as part of an eduSource Canada (http://www.edusource.ca/) initiative to create a network of interoperable learning object repositories across Canada. The ADLIB project proposes to integrate AU-developed learning objects, Digital Reading Room resources, and learning objects contributed by external users in a standardized, interoperable repository environment. The project aims to promote the sharing and reuse of digital learning resources among AU curriculum developers and the wider educational community.

ADLIB permits nonregistered users to browse, search, and view the contents of the repository. Registration is free, and an account permits users to upload learning objects or link to objects that are already online, to create simple or advanced metadata records that describe the objects, and to manage their own material. The ADLIB repository supports the Canadian Core Learning Resource Metadata Application Profile (CanCore; http://www.cancore.ca), a subset of the IEEE standard for Learning Object Metadata (LOM), customized for the Canadian educational sectors. Metadata, or "data about data" as it is commonly defined, is used to describe a learning object's characteristics, such as authorship, keywords, terms of distribution (free, cost, copyright), and pedagogical uses. Metadata is often compared to the library catalogue, which uses classification, subject cataloguing, and access points to aid users in locating relevant material. Metadata is what permits the object to be found when a user enters search terms into the database.

The technical aspects of learning objects and digital repositories can tend to overshadow in the literature the practical implications of teachers and learners using these resources. In a study to investigate barriers and facilitating factors affecting the use of learning objects, students enrolled in an AU Master of Distance Education course on instructional design were assigned the tasks of developing a learning object or incorporating learning objects into an instructional unit, posting their experiences with learning objects to a course discussion board, journaling the process, and submitting an essay on barriers and facilitating factors. The study found that facilitating factors included the availability of good examples of learning objects to serve as models and of online resources to provide information about the design, adaptation, and development of learning objects and to assist with the evaluation of learning objects. Barriers were more prevalent and included lack of a precise definition for "learning object," deficits in instructional design and technological skills, difficulties navigating and searching repositories, insufficient learning objects for some disciplines, poor-quality learning objects, imprecise definitions of granularity, concerns about ownership and attribution, and attitudinal barriers in the form of low confidence levels or willingness to share. The work involved in creating or repurposing a learning object was seen as challenging by some, but there was also an appreciation of the flexibility of learning objects and the climate of sharing that their use fostered (Moisey & Ally, 2004).

CONCLUSION

In this chapter we have described how electronic course reserves are streamlining the processes by which students access course-related materials, and how learning objects and online repositories are encouraging the discovery, sharing, and reuse of digital learning resources. These developments are transforming access to online educational materials for faculty and students in both traditional face-to-face and distance education environments. Libraries continue to perform their traditional role in linking users to materials, whether these are housed in virtual spaces or physical places, and now participate in the growing world of online scholarship and e-learning. Accessing, searching, retrieving, and using information resources from many different locations are not intuitive capabilities. As users grapple with learning digital library culture, a number of developments are promising to make digital libraries easier to use. In the next, and concluding, chapter, we look at some of the applications that are reducing the burden on the searcher by requiring the system to adapt to a more human approach to information seeking.

Beyond Digital Library Culture Barriers

In this book we have looked at the ways in which digital libraries are revolutionizing how scholars, teachers, and learners access and use research materials. We have also considered the changes in academic libraries, the relationships of information seekers to information sources, and the nature of scholarly communication. The information landscape has expanded to include resources such as electronic books, electronic journals, Web sites, electronic course reserves, and unique digital collections. Print culture remains a fundamental part of scholarship but it is enhanced by a digital culture that offers new opportunities to be creative with knowledge sources, to disseminate research and ideas, to engage learners, and to collaborate with colleagues.

Digital libraries are increasingly an integral component in the services traditional and distance or online education institutions offer their students and faculty. Successful participation in the world of scholarship requires an ability to interact with both print-based and digital research materials. Digital libraries have much to offer, but there are often barriers to overcome as researchers interact directly with unfamiliar, complex information systems that change frequently, offer an overwhelming amount of information, and seem to have a language of their own. Librarians are important resources in helping researchers work through the stresses and difficulties of interacting with unfamiliar digital library systems. Acculturation takes time as digital library users explore new information environments, develop an awareness of what is available, and learn the mechanics for effectively accessing relevant materials. Acquiring an understanding of digital libraries can help scholars become active participants as digital scholars and ensure that the needs of their academic discipline are met.

Digital libraries were not developed to make it more difficult to access information but rather to make it easier, to make valuable information available at the click of a mouse. Tell that to a student or academic who has spent hours searching for something on a library Web site without finding it! Early online information systems required the searcher to learn command languages and to race against the clock because charges were on the basis of connect times. Library users often relied on a librarian to carry out the search. Most online systems are now designed for end-user searching and have graphical user interfaces that are at least somewhat familiar to anyone who has searched the Web. However, there is a heavy burden on the user to think about online systems the way librarians and information scientists think about them. An effective online search requires an understanding of the contents, structure, and vocabulary of the particular database to which the inquiry is being directed, and most researchers need to learn to use more than one system. In this chapter we will look at ways in which the burden can be shifted from the searcher to the systems, so that the digital library more effectively meets the needs of its users and provides a friendlier online search environment.

HUMANS AND COMPUTERS INTERACTING

Digital libraries are not just about technology and digital objects—they are about the humans who interact with them. As Borgman (2003) observes, in the 1980s research into human-computer interaction emphasized the need for the user to adapt to the information system, with a focus on user training and the design of friendlier system interfaces, but people now have higher expectations because of the ubiquity of information and communication technologies. Users accustomed to single-purpose technologies such as automatic teller machines need to realize that some effort is required to use desktop computers, because the technology supports many different applications and the functionality cannot be readily inspected. The usability of information systems needs to improve, and these systems "will achieve wide acceptance only if they are easy to learn and use relative to perceived benefits" (Borgman, 2003, p. 86).

The screen display or interface design is central to the searcher's experience of an online system because it consists of the buttons, menus, and other features that are used in searching. Arms (2000) summarizes some general principles of interface design from recent research: "Consistency in appearance, in controls, and in function is important to users. Users need feedback; they need to understand what the computer system is doing and why they see certain results. They should be able to interrupt or reverse actions. Error handling should be simple and easy to comprehend. Skilled users should be offered shortcuts, while beginners should have simple, well-defined options. Above all, the user should feel in control" (p. 152). Some of the biggest challenges with interface design that users face is the variability from system to system and the continual updating of database interfaces, requiring users to relearn the system.

Functionality varies from database to database and includes options for limiting, sorting, and so on. Most online systems offer a choice between entering search terms or browsing a list of subjects. To formulate a query the searcher must brainstorm keywords, thinking of synonyms and related terms for the topic. Borgman observes that although it can be easy to get lost, browsing coincides more naturally with human behavior, as the searcher follows a visible path and recognizes the material that meets the information need. This is based on "two complementary principles of cognition": "people learn by making associations with prior knowledge" and "people usually find it easier to recognize information presented to them than to recall it from memory" (2000b, p. 158).

Designers of digital libraries need to be mindful not only of the underlying technology but of the sociological aspects, particularly the needs of the people who use digital libraries. Socially grounded research into digital libraries emphasizes relevance and usability of content for the community served, transparency so that users are not required to know the technology in order to use the system, and an understanding of the users and their work (Van House, Bishop, & Buttenfield, 2003).

Sometimes user needs may even be based in the spread of new technologies, such as the increased use of wireless devices and personal digital assistants (PDAs), and libraries need to address these emerging needs. For example, users of Palm handhelds with wireless access and mobile phones are accommodated by Millennium AirPAC, an online library catalogue designed by Innovative Interfaces Inc. AirPAC permits users to interact with the catalogue from any location accessible by wireless networks. John and Tucker (2003) point out that to support these users, librarians need to keep up-to-date with handheld technology, lobby information vendors for products that are designed for PDAs, and ensure library Web pages and online forms are compatible with PDA use. A growing number of libraries are offering handheld services, resources, and instruction. The University of Alberta Libraries, for example, offers PDA Zone (http://www.library.ualberta.ca/pdazone/). PDA users have access to a PDA infrared (IR) beaming station in the Health Sciences Library, which enables them to beam the results of database searches to their PDAs using infrared technology. They also have access to downloadable *Library News* via freely available AvantGo software, PDA instruction sessions, one-on-one consultations, the ua-pda listserv, wireless support, downloadable e-books, bibliographies, information databases, software, and PDA resource guides.

Digital libraries have the potential to create collaborative work environments, moving beyond simply providing access to information resources to providing an environment to support the work of a specific community (Lynch, 2003a). Academic digital libraries are usually passive, based on a "downstream" model in which users go to the library for information. David Robins (2002) describes a model in which users do not just "pull" information from the library; instead, the library operates on an upstream model and "pushes" information to the user. In the upstream model automated digital agents monitor information resources, match them to user profiles, and deliver them periodically to the user or user community. Digital libraries in this model have the potential to play an active role in information communities, delivering timely information resources, encouraging communication and collaboration, and growing along with their communities.

Meyyappan, Chowdhury, and Foo (2001) describe a digital work environment (DWE) prototype that permits searchers to access online resources through a personalized interface in which the resources are organized based on their relevance to the user's tasks. The DWE prototype was developed in the Division of Information Studies, School of Computer Engineering at Nanyang Technological University, Singapore. The proposed DWE "aims to provide users with the appropriate information needed to accomplish a particular task," without the user needing to know what information resources are available or needing to formulate a query (Meyyappan, Chowdhury, & Foo, 2001, p. 252). The user enters the system, identifies the particular task that needs to be accomplished, and the system, based on its knowledge about the user, the information resources, and the suitability of resources for particular tasks, takes the user directly to the appropriate resources for the task. The proposed DWE also provides a personal workspace for users to record and store information such as notes, references, publications, and favorite links.

Wikis represent a fascinating use of digital technology to support the goals of a community of users and are increasingly cropping up in educational contexts. *Wiki* is a Hawaiian word that means *quick* and is used to refer to "a website (or other hypertext document collection) that allows a user to add content, as on an Internet forum, but also allows that content to be edited by anyone" (Wikipedia, 2004). A wiki is comparable to a blog in that it is a form of groupware, but a key difference is that while readers can post comments to a blog, which is a chronological online journal of the thoughts and ideas of an individual or a group, a wiki is open to active collaboration from all invited users (Mattison, 2003). *Wikipedia, the Free Encyclopedia* (http://en.wikipedia.org), is one of the best-known wikis and permits anyone to edit its pages and build up its knowledge base. Wikis can be used in education to create an interactive online environment for instructors and students, enable access to course resources, provide a forum for discussion, develop a knowledge repository, and encourage democratic participation (Schwartz, Clark, Cossarin, & Rudolph, 2004). The potential for wiki use in libraries includes behind-the-scenes uses by librarians and public service uses for reader's advisory, patron suggestions, and frequently asked questions (Mattison, 2003). University of Winnipeg Library & Information Services introduced *What Would Batgirl Do?* (http://whatwouldbatgirldo.xwiki.com/) as an experimental wiki space that encourages questions and comments from students and permits students to change and add to the content.

Digital library users may carry out their work individually or as part of a community in entirely virtual spaces, or in the framework of a hybrid model in which they go to the library as a physical place and sit at computers to access the library's electronic environment. *Information commons* are a growing trend in academic libraries, providing well-designed physical settings in which students and faculty have access to top-notch computing equipment and the support of librarians, technology experts, and other professionals. Such environments support collaborative and individualized study, facilitate teaching and learning with technology, and foster opportunities for promoting information literacy. David Leighton describes the information commons at Pace University Library as follows:

> The Information Commons accommodates diverse learning styles, including formal classroom instruction, small group coaching, individual research consultation, and drop-in assistance. A hybrid skills team comprised of Reference and Instructional Librarians, Instructional Technologists, Student Technical Assistants, and Writing and Mathematics tutors provides a range of services within an organizational structure emphasizing inter-departmental coordination and distributed responsibility. Students are able to conduct research, obtain reference and tutorial assistance, write papers, tabulate data, design web-pages, develop e-portfolios, and collaborate in small groups on multimedia projects in a one-stop shopping mode. [2003, para. 2]

EASIER-TO-USE DIGITAL LIBRARIES

Providing facilitating environments in which digital library users can work, research, and learn is important, but users also need digital libraries that are user-friendly. Andrew K. Pace (2003) encourages librarians to learn from the service models employed by their for-profit sector Internet counterparts, such as Amazon's online bookstore (http://www.amazon.com). These dot-com services are often popular with Internet-savvy students because they make the online environment friendly and easy to use. Amazon provides a popular commercial example of how a digital library can personalize the search environment and build a user community. The online bookstore allows its users to specify their interests in order to receive personalized recommendations while logged in and to set up e-mail alerts. Amazon also has a "Customers who bought this book also bought..." feature to assist users in their selections, and it provides users with the opportunity to make recommendations, write online reviews, rate reviews, e-mail recommendations to their friends, create "wish lists," and build networks with other customers. The Amazon site includes a number of features that enhance the experience of searching a catalogue. There are book covers, tables of contents, editorial and customer reviews, a display of recent searches, easy-to-use subject searching, a "look inside" feature for previewing selected books, and the ability to search inside the full contents of selected books. Not surprisingly, library catalogues are beginning to emulate some of these features. For example, the Innovative Interfaces online public access catalogue offers a customization tool that includes a feature for users to build, save, and manage preferred searches and a Web-linking tool to enrich the catalogue content with features such as cover art, reviews, author biographies, online reference tools, and online bookstores. Increasingly, library catalogues are providing links to related resources and are using a shopping cart approach for users to request items. The library catalogue is evolving from a listing of holdings in a library's physical collection to a tool for integrating a library's physical and digital collections as well as external resources relevant to the community of users.

Many other developments are making digital libraries easier to use and offer hope for improved usability in the future, including linking and interoperability, personalized digital library environments, feedback functions, natural language processing, customer service software, and the Semantic Web.

Linking and Interoperability

Academic library Web sites usually offer a wide range of resources from which to choose. It can be particularly difficult to determine where to find a specific journal article in full text or which database to use for a particular research question. Some databases provide linking from the citation for an article to the full-text article in other databases. Libraries are also adding linking software to their Web sites. These link servers, or link resolvers, such as SFX from Ex Libris (http://www.exlibrisgroup.com/sfx.htm), streamline access to full-text documents. If an item is not available full text in the database the user is searching, the link server will point to other databases where it is available. When full text is not available online for the item, the link server can direct the searcher to library catalogues, document delivery, and interlibrary loans services. To locate a known article, the searcher enters bibliographic information about the item into the linker and is taken to the database where the item is located, and sometimes directly to the item itself.

Participating scholarly publishers have joined together in CrossRef, a not-for-profit network, to improve access to electronic resources. CrossRef aims to provide "an infrastructure for linking citations across publishers" based on the implementation of the Digital Object Identifier or DOI (CrossRef, 2003, para. 1).

A DOI is a string of letters and numbers that uniquely identifies an electronic resource and functions as a persistent, reliable link to that resource. When the searcher clicks on a CrossRef-linked resource, the link takes the searcher directly to the item regardless of where it is located. The searcher then has access to the resource through personal or institutional subscriptions or though pay-per-view options.

The most basic online search model requires a searcher to select a particular database and use the interface to search the database contents. The searcher must repeat this process for each database. Some database aggregators link their databases so that the searcher can select a number of databases offered through the aggregator, and search them simultaneously using the aggregator's interface. For example, if a library subscribes to a number of EBSCO databases, the searcher can opt to search some or all of these databases simultaneously.

Libraries are introducing federated search tools that permit the searcher to use a single interface to enter terms and run the search across multiple databases, regardless of who has produced the database. This helps solve the problem of users not knowing which database is most appropriate for a particular research problem. A federated search tool saves the searcher time, permitting a simultaneous search in different journal databases and other online resources such as library catalogues. Libraries can choose from a number of products such as MetaLib from Ex Libris (http://www.exlibrisgroup.com/metalib.htm) and MetaFind from Innovative Interfaces (http://www.iii.com/mill/digital.shtml). A comparable tool on the Web is the metasearch engine, such as MetaCrawler (http://www.metacrawler.com/), which searches the indexes of several search engines simultaneously.

The California Digital Library uses SearchLight (http://searchlight.cdlib.org/) to allow its community of users to run a search across the University of California databases and Internet resources and offers a public version that confines searching to the publicly available resources. The searcher types in keywords, and SearchLight performs the search in the different databases. SearchLight organizes the results by category, shows the number of items in each category, and ranks the results from most matches to least. Clicking on the results takes the searcher directly to the item or to a database to perform the search. SearchLight uses the Z39.50 protocol, an international standard that allows different computers to communicate with each other and a searcher in one system to search and retrieve information from other systems without needing to learn how to search the other systems. The Library of Congress, which is responsible for the maintenance of this standard, provides access to a Z39.50 Gateway (http://lcweb.loc.gov/z3950/gateway.html) to library catalogues around the world.

Personalized Digital Library Environments

Federated search tools reduce the number of places a searcher needs to look for information and the number of systems a searcher needs to learn. Personalized digital library environments streamline access to frequently used resources and create a friendlier online environment by permitting users to build their own digital collections in a personal workspace. Both these developments resolve some of the challenges digital library users face in accessing information resources that meet their needs.

Nanyang Technological University launched myNTU (http://www.ntu.edu.sg/) in 2003, an evolution of the earlier NTU digital library initiative GEMS (Gateway to Electronic Media Services), which was introduced in 1999, and the upgraded iGEMS version, which was introduced in 2001. myNTU offers the university's community a one-stop personalized approach to online services and resources: space to store and share online documents; newsletters delivered based on the user's selected preferences; a single interface for searching all of the online resources; the ability to save search criteria for future use; and tools to personalize the workspace in content and layout. Similar initiatives can be found at other institutions. For example, Cornell University Library offers MyLibrary (http://mylibrary.cornell.edu/MyLibrary/), a suite of electronic services that can be personalized to reflect the user's interests and research needs. It includes MyLinks to select, store, and organize electronic resources, and MyUpdates to set preferences to be periodically informed of new resources added to the library catalogue. A growing number of colleges and universities are implementing portal technology to foster a sense of community and permit users to customize their view of the institution's resources and services.

Feedback Functions

A search that comes back with "no items found" offers searchers no context in which to interpret why a particular search strategy has failed. Expert searchers know how to interpret results and refine searches. They will check spelling, adjust terminology, or revise the search statement in some other way. Less experienced searchers are more likely to assume that the information they need is not in the database and abandon the search. A search system that provides feedback promotes awareness of why some searches fail and enables searchers to make choices that will improve the effectiveness of a search. If you type the word "orangatan" into Google you will get some results because Web pages are full of spelling mistakes, but the search engine will return with a friendly "Did you mean: orang-utan?" If no documents are retrieved by a search, Google will provide suggestions such as "try different keywords" or "try more general keywords."

Library products are becoming more helpful in providing users with feedback and opportunities to adjust searches. If a search fails to retrieve items, some library catalogues are designed to show the searcher where the entry for the item would appear in a listing of nearby items, and offer other options for searching, such as changing a subject search to a keyword search. Journal database users are beginning to benefit from online help such as ProQuest's Smart Search, which analyzes the user's search and maps the terms to the database vocabulary. Smart Search asks, "Did you find what you're looking for?" and provides hyperlinks to suggested topics and publications for further searching. Such features can be especially useful when searching in an unfamiliar academic discipline. After the searcher selects a suggested topic, more suggestions are provided for narrowing the topic. Databases are also beginning to improve their communications with searchers through "what's new" pages and electronic newsletters, as well as by providing opportunities for searchers to e-mail suggestions and comments to the database provider.

Natural Language Processing

Most databases process search strings composed of characters and commands, such as Boolean operators, in a very literal and unforgiving manner, and the burden is on the searcher to interpret how the computer will understand the query. However, some systems use natural language processing to recognize meaning and manipulate queries in the context of human language. When a system uses natural language processing, searchers can express their queries in the same way they would ask a question or speak to someone. For example, in a system capable of handling natural language queries a searcher could enter *What are the differences between monkeys and apes?* rather than *difference* and monkey* and (ape* or chimpanzee* or gorilla*)*. The system uses complex algorithms to determine the searcher's information need. The AskJeeves search engine (http://www.ask.com/) specializes in natural language queries, and some databases producers, such as ProQuest, offer natural language searching. A natural language search option can help searchers who need to find information quickly, but searchers who require more exhaustive search results may find that natural language searching does not give them enough control over their searches.

Customer Service Software

SmarterChild (http://www.smarterchild.com/) is an interactive automated agent developed by Conversagent, Inc. that interacts with users over text messaging systems such as AOL's Instant Messenger. SmarterChild responds to natural language questions about news headlines, sports scores, Shakespeare, U.S. presidents, and other topics, engaging users in conversation. The Conversagent technology represents a self-service model in which customers ask questions of agents or "bots" and receive automated replies. The interaction is limited to easy-to-resolve queries, and questions of a more in-depth nature need to be referred to a live customer service representative.

Some companies on the Internet are using customer relation management (CRM) software to respond in real time to customer queries. These services use chat to enable customers to communicate with human agents and cobrowsing to enable the customer service representative to use the customer's Web browser to do a walk-through of a Web site. This technology has become popular with libraries establishing digital reference services. The Open University Library UK (http://library.open.ac.uk/) uses LivePerson software to power its "Librarians on Call" service as a means of providing live online assistance to its distance learning community. A wide range of libraries in North America have joined in national and private cooperatives to offer real-time online reference services using 24/7 Reference software (http://www.247ref.org/). These and similar products can help librarians interact with users who are accessing the library at a distance. Cobrowsing is especially useful because it enables the researcher to see how the librarian is navigating through online resources. Of course, some queries require more in-depth follow-up, and libraries are usually positioned to provide alternate methods for providing reference services to remote users, such as toll-free telephone and e-mail.

The Semantic Web

Tim Berners-Lee, known for his work in developing the World Wide Web, proposes the development of a Semantic Web, which as an extension of the current Web "will bring structure to the meaningful content of Web pages, creating an environment where software agents roaming from page to page can readily carry out sophisticated tasks for users" (Berners-Lee, Hendler, & Lassila, 2001, para. 7). Whereas the current Web is designed for computers to display data that human beings read, the Semantic Web will make sense to computers, permitting them to unravel the complexities of human language, make connections among pages, and deliver up useful information to human users. This ability of computers to make sense of human information will be based on the coding of Web documents with metadata, the use of a language to structure data, the use of ontologies to define relations among terms, and the implementation of digital signatures to ensure the authenticity of Web documents.

CONCLUSION

The online information environment can be made more responsive to the needs of researchers through the further development and implementation of friendlier, more consistent system interfaces that accommodate a variety of users and information needs, federated search tools that save searchers time and frustration, tools for customizing the search environment, feedback about what has gone wrong with a search and how to improve it, natural language processing, chat, and cobrowsing tools. The Semantic Web, currently only in a formative stage, holds out the promise that the Web will one day offer a more automated approach to information delivery. Improving the technology is crucial to improving the effectiveness of digital libraries, but human interaction and collaboration are also important.

Whether teaching and learning occur in campus-based environments or in virtual universities, students and faculty are using digital libraries with increasing frequency and librarians are taking on new roles in guiding this exploration. We hope this book has been a helpful guide along the way to learning about digital library culture and that readers will feel comfortable in seeking out the assistance of both their live and virtual librarians. Librarians continue to play an essential role in supporting students and faculty as they explore digital libraries and the world of digital scholarship.

Librarian roles in supporting digital scholarship are many:

• Research, develop, evaluate, and implement digital libraries.

• Select and organize electronic information resources into information gateways.

• Develop and provide access to unique digital collections.

- Promote awareness of available online resources through subject listings of resources, newsletters, "what's new" pages, and so forth.
- Provide technical support to users accessing online resources.
- Connect with remote users and distance learners through virtual reference services.
- Contribute to digital preservation initiatives and work institutionally to ensure procedures are in place.
- Ensure continued access to valuable print materials.
- Negotiate licensing agreements with publishers and vendors of online information resources.
- Work in consortia and take advantage of consortial subscription offers to increase availability of online resources.
- Communicate the needs of users to database aggregators and online publishers.
- Provide tutorials and other instruction for online research.
- Contribute to learning object initiatives and share metadata expertise.
- Work with faculty to develop student information literacy initiatives and to integrate them into the curriculum.
- Support scholarly electronic publishing and open access initiatives and raise awareness of the benefits.
- Keep current with the information technology marketplace.

Appendix: Web Resources

What follows is a chapter-by-chapter alphabetical listing of the Web resources referred to in this book. Given the nature of the online environment we cannot guarantee the stability of the links, but if you find that a particular URL is not working try typing the name of the site into a search engine.

CHAPTER ONE

Academic Info—digital libraries, online publications, exhibits, documents, and journals (http://www.academicinfo.net/digital.html)

ACM Digital Library (http://www.acm.org/dl/)

BookCrossing (http://www.bookcrossing.com)

California Digital Library (CDL; http://www.cdlib.org/)

Canadian Initiative on Digital Libraries (http://www.collectionscanada.ca/cidl/)

Cuneiform Digital Library Initiative (CDLI; http://cdli.ucla.edu/)

Delos Network of Excellence on Digital Libraries (http://delos-noe.iei.pi.cnr.it/)

Digital Libraries Initiative, Phase 1 (http://www.dli2.nsf.gov/dlione/)

Digital Libraries Initiative, Phase 2 (http://www.dli2.nsf.gov/)

Digital Library Federation (http://www.diglib.org/)

Electronic Libraries (eLib) Programme (http://www.ukoln.ac.uk/services/elib/)

International Council for Open and Distance Education (http://www.icde.org/)

Library of Congress (http://www.loc.gov/)

Library of Congress American Memory project (http://memory.loc.gov)

Library of Congress Digital Collections & Programs (http://www.loc.gov/library/libarch-digital.html)

Library of Congress Global Gateway (http://international.loc.gov/intldl/intldlhome.html)

Library of Congress Prints and Photographs Online Catalog (http://www.loc.gov/rr/print/catalog.html)

Library of Congress THOMAS (http://thomas.loc.gov/)

New Zealand Digital Library (http://www.nzdl.org/fast-cgi-bin/library?a=p&p=home)

Peterson's Distance Learning (http://www.petersons.com/distancelearning/)

World Wide Learn (http://www.worldwidelearn.com/)

CHAPTER TWO

ArXiv.org e-Print Archive (http://arxiv.org/)

Athabasca University Bazaar Online Conference System (http://klaatu.pc.athabascau.ca/)

Bailey, C. W. *Scholarly Electronic Publishing Bibliography* (http://info.lib.uh.edu/sepb/sepb.html)

BioMed Central (http://www.biomedcentral.com/)

CogPrints (http://cogprints.ecs.soton.ac.uk/)

Create Change (http://www.createchange.org/)

Creative Commons (http://creativecommons.org/)

Directory of Open Access Journals (http://www.doaj.org/)

H-Net Humanities and Social Sciences Online (http://www.h-net.org/)

Humanities Text Initiative (http://www.hti.umich.edu/)

International Consortium for the Advancement of Academic Publication (ICAAP; http://www.icaap.org/portal/)

International Review of Research in Open and Distance Learning (*IRRODL*; http://www.irrodl.org/)

Journal of Insect Science (http://www.insectscience.org)

JSTOR (http://www.jstor.com) subscription

MIT OpenCourseWare (http://ocw.mit.edu/index.html)

Moodle (http://moodle.org)

Networked Digital Library of Theses and Dissertations (NDLTD; http://www.ndltd.org/)

Nineteenth-Century Art Worldwide (*NCAW*; http://19thc-artworldwide.org/)

Online Medieval and Classical Library (http://sunsite.berkeley.edu/OMACL/)

OYEZ Project (http://www.oyez.org/oyez/frontpage)

Project Gutenberg (http://gutenberg.net/)

Project Muse (http://muse.jhu.edu./) subscription

Public Library of Science (PLoS; http://www.publiclibraryofscience.org/)

Sakai (www.sakaiproject.org)

Scholarly Publishing and Academic Resources Coalition (SPARC; http://www.arl.org/sparc/)

Ulrich's Periodicals Directory (http://ulrichsweb.com/ulrichsweb/) subscription

University of California eScholarship Repository (http://repositories.cdlib.org/escholarship/)

WoPEc (http://netec.mcc.ac.uk/WoPEc.html)

CHAPTER THREE

Athabasca University *Course Authors Guide* (http://emd.athabascau.ca/resources/course_authors_guide_jun03.pdf)

Athabasca University *The Insider* (http://www.athabascau.ca/insider/)

Athabasca University Library Digital Reference Centre (http://library.athabascau.ca/drc.php)

Athabasca University Library Help Centre (http://library.athabascau.ca/help.php)

Athabasca University Library Links by Subject (http://library.athabascau.ca/link.php)

Athabasca University Student Union *The Voice* (http://www.ausu.org/voice/)

Canadian Universities Reciprocal Borrowing Agreement (http://www.coppul.ca/rb/rbindex.html)

Francoeur, S. *The Teaching Librarian* (http://www.teachinglibrarian.org/digref.htm)

Georgetown University Library Ask a Librarian (http://gulib.lausun.georgetown.edu/resource/chat.htm)

HumanClick (http://www.humanclick.com/)

Library and Archives Canada Digital Collections (http://www.collectionscanada.ca)

Library of Congress American Memory project (http://memory.loc.gov)

Live Assistance (http://www.liveassistance.com/)

Live Person (http://www.liveperson.com/)

Open University UK Routes (http://routes.open.ac.uk/)

Penn State Libraries Online Reference Resources (http://www.libraries.psu.edu/gateway/referenceshelf/).

Sloan, B. *Digital Reference Services Bibliography* (http://www.lis.uiuc.edu/~b-sloan/digiref.html)

The Alberta Library (TAL; http://www.thealbertalibrary.ab.ca)

University College Dublin subject portals (http://www.ucd.ie/library/subject_portals/index.html)

University of California Berkeley Libraries Finding Information (http://www.lib.berkeley.edu/Help/finding_information.html)

University of California Irvine Libraries Online Reference Resources (http://www.lib.uci.edu/online/reference/reference.html)

University of Maryland University College Chat with a Librarian (http://polaris.umuc.edu/library/liveassistance/patronform.html).

University of Southern California Teaching and Learning with Technology Conference (http://www.usc.edu/isd/locations/cst/tls/events/tlt2004/)

CHAPTER FOUR

Association of College & Research Libraries (ACRL) *Information Literacy Assessment Issues* (http://www.ala.org/ala/acrl/acrlissues/acrlinfolit/infolitresources/infolitassess/assessment issues.htm)

California State University Information Competency Program (http://www.calstate.edu/LS/Aboutinfocomp.shtml)

CUNY Bilingual Information Competency Tutorial (http://www.hostos.cuny.edu/library/HHCL_New_Web/New_Spanish_Tutorial/revised/tutorialespanol/Index.html)

Georgia State University World History Seminar (http://www.library.gsu.edu/world history/home.htm)

Indiana University Bloomington Libraries Information Literacy Assessment Plan (http://www.indiana.edu/~libinstr/Information_Literacy/assessment.html)

Information Literacy at Florida International University (FIU; http://www.fiu.edu/~library/ili/index.html)

International Federation of Library Associations and Institutions (IFLA) *Guidelines for Information Literacy Assessment* (http://www.ifla.org/VII/s42/pub/IL-guidelines 2004-e.pdf)

National Higher Education ICT (Information and Communication Technology) Initiative (http://www.ets.org/ictliteracy)

Project SAILS (http://sails.lms.kent.edu/index.php)

University of California Los Angeles Bruin Success with Less Stress (http://www.library.ucla.edu/bruinsuccess/)

University of Louisville Libraries Information Literacy Program (http://www.louisville.edu/infoliteracy/)

University of Massachusetts Amherst Instructional Services (http://www.library.umass.edu/instruction/instructservices.html)

University of Massachusetts Amherst MERLIN (http://www.library.umass.edu/merlin/)

University of Texas System Digital Library TILT (http://tilt.lib.utsystem.edu/)

Washington State Assessment of Information and Technology Literacy (http://depts.washington.edu/infolitr/)

CHAPTER FIVE

ABI/Inform (http://www.proquest.com) subscription

Academic Search Premier (http://www.ebsco.com) subscription

Acadia University You Quote It, You Note It (http://library.acadiau.ca/tutorials/plagiarism/)

Arts & Humanities Citation Index (http://isi01.isiknowledge.com/portal.cgi/) subscription

Blackwell Synergy (http://www.blackwellsynergy.com) subscription

Cumulative Index to Nursing & Allied Literature (CINAHL) subscription

EndNote (http://www.endnote.com/)

Expanded Academic ASAP (http://www.gale.com) subscription

Google Scholar (http://scholar.google.com/)

Humbul Humanities Hub (http://www.humbul.ac.uk/)

JSTOR (http://www.jstor.com) subscription

MEDLINE subscription

Oxford Reference Online (http://www.oxfordreference.com) subscription

Oxford University Bodleian Library Broadside Ballads (http://www.bodley.ox.ac.uk/ballads/ballads.htm)

Plagiarism & Academic Integrity at Rutgers University (http://www.scc.rutgers.edu/douglass/sal/plagiarism/intro.html)

ProCite (http://www.procite.com/)

PSIgate-Physical Sciences Information Gateway (http://www.psigate.ac.uk/newsite/)

PsycINFO subscription

Questia (http://www.questia.com)

Reference Manager (http://www.refman.com/)

Science Citation Index (http://isi01.isiknowledge.com/portal.cgi/) subscription

Sherman, C., and Price, G. *The Invisible Web Directory* (http://invisible-web.net/)

Social Science Information Gateway (SOSIG; http://www.sosig.ac.uk/)

Social Sciences Citation Index (http://isi01.isiknowledge.com/portal.cgi/) subscription

Sociological Abstracts subscription

Statistical Universe (http://www.lexis-nexis.com/) subscription

Turnitin (http://www.turnitin.com)

University of California Digital Scriptorium (http://sunsite.berkeley.edu/scriptorium/)

University of Texas Austin Digital Morphology (http://www.digimorph.org/)

University of Texas System UT System Crash Course in Copyright (http://www.utsystem.edu/ogc/ intellectualproperty/cprtindx.htm)

University of Toronto Libraries Discovery and Early Development of Insulin (http://digital.library.utoronto.ca/insulin/)

Wilson OmniFile (http://www.hwwilson.com/) subscription

xreferplus (http://www.xreferplus.com) subscription

CHAPTER SEVEN

Athabasca University Library Digital Reference Centre (http://library.athabascau.ca/drc.php)

Athabasca University Library Help Centre (http://library.athabascau.ca/help.php)

Athabasca University Library *MAIS Research Guide* (http://library.athabascau.ca/help/mais/main.htm)

Athabasca University Library *Psychology Research Guide* (http://library.athabascau.ca/help/psyc/introduction.htm)

Encyclopedia Britannica Online (http://www.britannica.com/) subscription

Oxford University Press *Oxford English Dictionary Online* (http://www.oed.com/) subscription

CHAPTER EIGHT

Athabasca University ADLIB (http://adlib.athabascau.ca/)

Athabasca University Library Digital Reading Room (http://library.athabascau.ca/drr/)

Campus Alberta Repository of Educational Objects (CAREO; http://www.careo.org/)

Canadian Core Learning Resource Metadata Application Profile (CanCore; http://www.cancore.ca)

eduSource Canada (http://www.edusource.ca/)

Multimedia Educational Resource for Learning and Online Teaching (MERLOT; http://www.merlot.org/)

University of Wisconsin System Institute for Global Studies (http://www.uw-igs.org/)

Wisconsin Online Resource Center (http://www.wisc-online.com/)

CHAPTER NINE

24/7 Reference (http://www.247ref.org/)

Amazon.com (http://www.amazon.com)

AskJeeves (http://www.ask.com/)

California Digital Library SearchLight (http://searchlight.cdlib.org/)

Cornell University Library MyLibrary (http://mylibrary.cornell.edu/MyLibrary/)

Ex Libris MetaLib (http://www.exlibrisgroup.com/metalib.htm)

Ex Libris SFX (http://www.exlibrisgroup.com/sfx.htm)

Innovative Interfaces MetaFind (http://www.iii.com/mill/digital.shtml)

Library of Congress Z39.50 Gateway (http://lcweb.loc.gov/z3950/gateway.html)

MetaCrawler (http://www.metacrawler.com/)

Nanyang Technological University myNTU (http://www.ntu.edu.sg/)

Open University Library UK Librarians on Call (http://library.open.ac.uk/)

SmarterChild (http://www.smarterchild.com/)

University of Alberta Libraries PDA Zone (http://www.library.ualberta.ca/pdazone/)

UWinnipeg Library & Information Services *What Would Batgirl Do?* (http://whatwouldbatgirldo.xwiki.com/)

Wikipedia, the Free Encyclopedia (http://en.wikipedia.org)

References

Adams, K. E., & Cassner, M. (2001). Marketing library resources and services to distance faculty. In A. M. Casey (Ed.), *Off-campus library services* (pp. 5–22). Binghamton, NY: Haworth Information Press.

American Library Association. (1989). *Presidential Committee on Information Literacy: Final report.* Retrieved July 1, 2004, from http://www.ala.org/ala/acrl/acrlpubs/white papers/presidential.htm

Andersen, D. L. (2004). Introduction. In D. L. Andersen (Ed.), *Digital scholarship in the tenure, promotion, and review process* (pp. 3–24). Armonk, NY: Sharpe.

Anderson, T., & Elloumi, F. (2004). Introduction. In T. Anderson & F. Elloumi (Eds.), *Theory and practice of online learning* (pp. xv–xxvi). Athabasca, AB: Athabasca University. Retrieved August 13, 2004, from http://cde.athabascau.ca/online_book/

Arms, W. Y. (2000). *Digital libraries (Digital libraries and electronic publishing).* Cambridge, MA: MIT Press.

Association of College & Research Libraries (ACRL). (2000). *Information literacy competency standards for higher education.* Retrieved August 13, 2004, from http://www.ala.org/ala/acrl/acrlstandards/informationliteracycompetency.htm

Association of College & Research Libraries (ACRL). (2002). *Information literacy standards toolkit. Standard five.* Retrieved August 13, 2004, from http://archive.ala.org/acrl/il/toolkit/five/five.html

Association of College & Research Libraries (ACRL). (2003). *Accreditation: Information literacy and accreditation agencies.* Retrieved February 1, 2005, from http://www.ala.org/ala/acrl/acrlissues/acrlinfolit/infolitstandards/infolitaccred/accreditation.htm

Association of College & Research Libraries (ACRL). (2004). *Guidelines for distance learning library services.* Chicago: American Library Association. Retrieved August 13, 2004, from http://www.ala.org/ala/acrl/acrlstandards/guidelinesdistancelearning.htm

Association of Research Libraries (ARL). (1996). *Transforming libraries. Issues and innovations in . . . Electronic reserves.* Retrieved August 13, 2004, from http://www.arl.org/transform/eres/index.html

Athabasca University. (2002). *Strategic university plan, 2002–2006.* Retrieved August 13, 2004, from http://www.athabascau.ca/sup/sup_19_06.pdf

Athabasca University, Institutional Studies. (2004). *Report on student usage and satisfaction with Athabasca University Library services, 2004.* Retrieved December 13, 2004, from http://library.athabascau.ca/about/report04.pdf

Bailey, C. W. (1996–2004). *Scholarly electronic publishing bibliography.* Houston: University of Houston Libraries. Retrieved August 13, 2004, from http://info.lib.uh.edu/sepb/sepb.html

Behr, M. D. (2004). On ramp to research: Creation of a multimedia library instruction presentation for off-campus students. In P. B. Mahoney (Ed.), *Eleventh off-campus library services conference proceedings* (pp. 13–20). Mount Pleasant: Central Michigan University.

Bennett, J., & Bennett, L. (2003). A review of factors that influence the diffusion of innovation when structuring a faculty training program. *The Internet and Higher Education, 6,* 53–63. Retrieved August 22, 2004, from *Science Direct* database.

Bergman, M. K. (2001). The Deep Web: Surfacing hidden value. *Journal of Electronic Publishing, 7*(1). Retrieved August 13, 2004, from http://www.press.umich.edu/jep/07-01/bergman.html

Berners-Lee, T., Hendler, J., & Lassila, O. (2001, May). The Semantic Web. *Scientific American.* Retrieved August 22, 2004, from http://www.sciam.com/article.cfm?articleID=00048144–10D2–1C70–84A9809EC588EF21

Bontenbal, K. F. (2000). Challenges faced by reference librarians in familiarizing adult students with the computerized library of today: The Cuesta College experience. In K. Sarkodie-Mensah (Ed.), *Reference services for the adult learner: Challenging issues for the traditional and technological era* (pp. 69–76). Binghamton, NY: Haworth Press.

Borgman, C. (1999). What are digital libraries? Competing visions. *Information Processing and Management, 35*(3), 227–43. Retrieved August 13, 2004, from *Science Direct* database.

Borgman, C. (2000a). Digital libraries and the continuum of scholarly communication. *Journal of Documentation, 56*(4), 412–30.

Borgman, C. (2000b). *From Gutenberg to the global information infrastructure: Access to information in the networked world.* Cambridge, MA: MIT Press.

Borgman, C. (2003). Designing digital libraries for usability. In A. P. Bishop, N. A. Van House, & B. P. Buttenfield (Eds.), *Digital library use: Social practice in design and evaluation* (pp. 85–118). Cambridge, MA: MIT Press.

Breivik, P. Senn, & Gee, E. G. (1989). *Information literacy: Revolution in the library.* Upper Saddle River, NJ: Macmillan.

Brod, C. (1984). *Technostress: The human cost of the computer revolution.* Reading, MA: Addison-Wesley.

Bush, V. (1945). As we may think. *The Atlantic Monthly.* Retrieved June 10, 2004, from http://www.theatlantic.com/unbound/flashbks/computer/bushf.htm [Requires subscription]

California Digital Library (CDL). (2005). *Home page.* The Regents of the University of California. Retrieved August 13, 2004, from http://www.cdlib.org/

California State University. (1985). *The mission of the California State University.* Retrieved July 1, 2004, from http://www.calstate.edu/PA/info/mission.shtml

California State University. (1995). *Information competence at CSU: A report.* Retrieved July 1, 2004, from http://www.calstate.edu/LS/Archive/info_comp_report.pdf

Cawthorne, J. E. (2003, November). Integrating outreach and building partnerships: Expanding our role in the learning community. *College & Research Library News, 666–669.*

Chowdhury, G. G., & Chowdhury, S. (2002). *Introduction to digital libraries.* London: Library Association.

Convey, J. (1992). *Online information retrieval. An introductory manual to principles and practice* (4th ed.). London: Library Association Publishing.

Cook, D. (2000). Creating connections: A review of the literature. In D. Raspa & D. Ward (Eds.), *The collaborative imperative: Librarians and faculty working together in the information universe* (pp. 19–38). Chicago: Association of College & Research Libraries.

Create Change. (2000). *About Create Change.* Retrieved August 13, 2004, from http://www.createchange.org/librarians/intro/aboutcc.html

CrossRef. (2003). *FastFacts.* Retrieved August 13, 2004, from http://www.crossref.org/01company/16fastfacts.html

Cuneiform Digital Library Initiative (CDLI). (2004). *About CDLI.* Retrieved August 13, 2004, from http://cdli.ucla.edu/about.html

Currie, C. L. (2000). Facilitating adult learning: The role of the academic librarian. In K. Sarkodie-Mensah (Ed.), *Reference services for the adult learner: Challenging issues for the traditional and technological era* (pp. 219–231). Binghamton, NY: Haworth Press.

Curzon, S. C. (2004). Developing faculty-librarian partnerships in information literacy. In I. F. Rockman (Ed.), *Integrating information literacy into the higher education curriculum: Practical models for transformation* (pp. 29–45). San Francisco: Jossey-Bass.

Dialog. (2004). *Gale directory of online, portable, and Internet databases.* Retrieved August 13, 2004, from http://library.dialog.com/bluesheets/html/bl0230.html

Digital Library Federation. (2005). *Home page.* Retrieved March 23, 2005, from http://www.diglib.org/

Dinwiddie, M., & Lillard, L. L. (2002). At the crossroads: Library and classroom. *Journal of Library Administration, 37*(1/2), 251–267.

Doskatch, I. (2003). Perceptions and perplexities of the faculty-librarian partnership: An Australian perspective. *Reference Services Review, 31*(2), 111–121. Retrieved August 22, 2004, from *Emerald FullText* database.

DSpace Federation. (2003). *Home page.* Cambridge, MA: MIT Libraries & Hewlett-Packard. Retrieved August 13, 2004, from http://www.dspace.org

Educational Testing Service (ETS). (2004). *ETS collaborates with major universities to assess 21st century skills.* Retrieved December 2, 2004, from http://www.ets.org/ictliteracy/educator.html

Eisenberg, M. B., Lowe, C. A., & Spitzer, K. L. (2004). *Information literacy: Essential skills for the information age* (2nd ed.). Westport, CT: Libraries Unlimited.

Friedlander, A. (2002, November). *Dimensions and use of the scholarly information environment* (Tables 17, 20). Retrieved August 13, 2004, from http://www.clir.org/pubs/reports/pub110/contents.html

Gaide, S. (2004, April 15). Integrated library services boosts online recruitment and retention. *Distance Education Report, 8*(8), 1–2, 6. Retrieved August 22, 2004, from *Academic Search Premier* database.

Gandhi, S. (2003). Academic librarians and distance education: Challenges and opportunities. *Reference & User Services Quarterly, 43*(2), 138–154.

Gapen, D. K. (1993). The virtual library: Knowledge, society, and the librarian. In L. M. Saunders (Ed.), *The virtual library: Visions and realities* (pp. 1–14). Westport, CT: Meckler.

Gere, C. (2002). *Digital culture.* London: Reaktion Books.

Ginsparg, P. (2003, March 13). *Can peer review be better focused?* Retrieved August 13, 2004, from http://arxiv.org/blurb/pg02pr.html

Gismondi, M., Johnson, K., Ross, L., & Tin, T. (2005). *An evaluation of the impact of the Digital Reading Room (DRR) on faculty, library, and educational media development staff and students: Final report.* Athabasca, AB: Athabasca University.

Google. (2004). *Corporate information: Technology overview.* Retrieved August 13, 2004, from http://www.google.ca/corporate/tech.html

Gorman, M. (2003). *The enduring library: Technology, tradition, and the quest for balance.* Chicago: American Library Association.

Grimes, D. J., & Boening, C. H. (2001). Worries with the Web: A look at student use of Web resources. *College & Research Libraries, 62*(1), 11–23. Retrieved August 13, 2004, from *Wilson OmniFile* database.

Heller-Ross, H. (1996, Summer). Librarian and faculty partnerships for distance education. *MC Journal: The Journal of Academic Media Librarianship, 4*(1). Retrieved July 8, 2004, from http://wings.buffalo.edu/publications/mcjrnl/v4n1/platt.html

Herring, S. (2001). Using the World Wide Web for research: Are faculty satisfied? *Journal of Academic Librarianship, 27*(3), 213–219. Retrieved August 13, 2004, from *Academic Search Premier* database.

Hollar, S., Sutch, L., & Nichols, D. (2001). Powerful partnerships: Cross-campus collaboration for faculty instructional technology education. In B. I. Dewey (Ed.), *Library user education: Powerful learning, powerful partnerships* (pp. 113–119). Lanham, MD: Scarecrow Press.

Houbeck, R. L. (2002). Leveraging our assets: The academic library and campus leadership. *The bottom line: Managing library finances, 15*(2), 54–59. Retrieved August 22, 2004, from *Emerald FullText* database.

Howell, S. L., Saba, F., Lindsay, N. K., & Williams, P. B. (2004). Seven strategies for enabling faculty success in distance education. *Internet and Higher Education, 7,* 33–49.

Hufford, J. R. (2000). The university library's role in planning a successful distance learning program. In K. Sarkodie-Mensah (Ed.), *Reference services for the adult learner: Challenging issues for the traditional and technological era* (pp. 193–203). Binghamton, NY: Haworth Press.

Jeffries, S. (2000). The librarian as networker: Setting the standard for higher education. In D. Raspa & D. Ward (Eds.), *The collaborative imperative: Librarians and faculty working together in the information universe* (pp. 114–129). Chicago: Association of College & Research Libraries.

John, N. R., & Tucker, D. C. (2003). 10 myths about PDAs—Debunked! *Computers in Libraries, 23*(3), 26–30. Retrieved December 13, 2004, from *Academic Search Premier* database.

Johnson, K., Trabelsi, H., & Tin, T. (2004). Library support for online learners: E-resources, e-services, and the human factors. In T. Anderson & F. Elloumi (Eds.), *Theory and practice of online learning* (pp. 349–365). Athabasca, AB: Athabasca University. Retrieved August 16, 2004, from http://cde.athabascau.ca/online_book/

JSTOR. (2004). *JSTOR's electronic-archiving initiative.* Retrieved August 13, 2004, from http://www.jstor.org/about/earchive.html

Kelley, K. B., & Orr, G. J. (2003, May). Trends in distance student use of electronic resources: A survey. *College & Research Libraries, 64*(3), 176–191. Retrieved August 22, 2004, from http://www.ala.org/ACRLtemplate.cfm?Section=january031&Template=/Members Only.cfm&ContentFileID=22620

Kennedy, D., & Duffy, T. (2004, June). Collaboration: A key principle in distance education. *Open Learning, 19*(2), 203–211.

Kennedy, S., & Price, G. (2004, November 18). Big news: "Google Scholar" is born. *ResourceShelf.* Retrieved December 29, 2004, from http://www.resourceshelf.com/2004/11/wow-its-google-scholar.html

Kling, R., & McKim, G. (1999, March 22). *Scholarly communication and the continuum of electronic publishing.* Bloomington: Center for Social Informatics, Indiana University School of Library and Information Science. Retrieved August 13, 2004, from http://arxiv.org/abs/cs.CY/9903015 [Preprint version of the article subsequently published in *Journal of the American Society for Information Science, 50*(10), 1999, 890–906]

Kupersmith, J. (1998). Technostress in the bionic library. In C. M. LaGuardia (Ed.), *Recreating the academic library: Breaking virtual ground* (pp. 23–47). New York: Neal-Schuman.

Large, A., Tedd, L. A., & Hartley, R. J. (1999). *Information seeking in the online age: Principles and practice.* London: Bowker.

Leighton, D. (2003, Fall). The information commons: A conceptualisation and vision for collaborative & interactive learning. *The Information Edge, 8*(1). Retrieved December 13, 2004, from http://www.pace.edu/library/pages/newsletter/fall2003/information-commons.html

Licklider, J.C.R. (1965). *Libraries of the future.* Cambridge, MA: MIT Press.

Lillard, L. L., Wilson, P., & Baird, C. M. (2004). Progressive partnering: Expanding student and faculty access to information services. In P. B. Mahoney (Ed.), *Eleventh off-campus library services conference proceedings* (pp. 169–180). Mount Pleasant: Central Michigan University.

Littlejohn, A. (2003). Issues in reusing online resources. In A. Littlejohn (Ed.), *Reusing online resources: A sustainable approach to e-learning* (pp. 1–6). London: Kogan Page.

Lynch, C. (2003a). Colliding with the real world: Heresies and unexplored questions about audience, economics, and control of digital libraries. In A. P. Bishop, N. A. Van House, & B. P. Buttenfield (Eds.), *Digital library use: Social practice in design and evaluation* (pp. 191–216). Cambridge, MA: MIT Press.

Lynch, L. (2003b, June). Interview with Jerry Goldman. *Creative Commons.* Retrieved August 13, 2004, from http://creativecommons.org/getcontent/features/oyez

Mattison, D. (2003). Quickiwiki, Swiki, Twiki, Zwiki, and the Plone Wars. *Searcher, 11*(4), 32–48. Retrieved December 13, 2004, from *Academic Search Premier* database.

Meldrem, J. A., Johnson, C., & Spradling, C. (2001). Navigating knowledge together: Faculty-librarian partnerships in Web-based learning. In B. I. Dewey (Ed.), *Library user education: Powerful learning, powerful partnerships* (pp. 30–36). Lanham, MD: Scarecrow Press.

Meszaros, R. L. (2002). The Internet, scholarly communication, and collaborative research. In C. F. Thomas (Ed.), *Libraries, the Internet, and scholarship: Tools and trends converging* (pp. 31–44). New York: Marcel Dekker.

Meyyappan, N., Chowdhury, G. G., & Foo, S. (2001). Use of a digital work environment prototype to create a user-centered university digital library. *Journal of Information Science, 27*(4), 249–264.

Middle States Commission on Higher Education (MSCHE). (2002). *Characteristics for excellence in higher education: Eligibility requirements and standards for accreditation.* Philadelphia: Middle States Commission on Higher Education.

Middle States Commission on Higher Education (MSCHE). (2003). *Developing research and communication skills: Guidelines for information literacy in the curriculum.* Philadelphia: Middle States Commission on Higher Education.

Moisey, S., & Ally, M. (2004, June). *Factors affecting the use of learning objects.* Paper presented at the Canadian Association for Distance Education Conference, Toronto, Ontario.

Mouat, J. (2003, June). *Crossing our own borders: Partnerships with librarians and instructional designers in the online environment.* Paper presented at the joint conference of the

American Library Association and the Canadian Library Association, Toronto, Ontario. Retrieved March 23, 2005, from http://www.athabascau.ca/courses/infs/200/unit04.html

National Center for Education Statistics. (2004). *Contexts of postsecondary education. Learning opportunities. Indicator 32.* Retrieved August 13, 2004, from http://nces.ed.gov/programs/coe/2004/section5/indicator32.asp

National Telecommunications and Information Administration (NTIA) and the Economics and Statistics Administration. (2002a, February). Chapter 1: Overview. In *A nation online: How Americans are expanding their use of the Internet.* Washington, DC: Author. Retrieved August 13, 2004, from http://www.ntia.doc.gov/ntiahome/dn/html/Chapter1.htm

National Telecommunications and Information Administration (NTIA) and the Economics and Statistics Administration. (2002b, February). Chapter 5: The digital generation: How young people have embraced computers and the Internet. In *A nation online: How Americans are expanding their use of the Internet.* Washington, DC: Author. Retrieved August 13, 2004, from http://www.ntia.doc.gov/ntiahome/dn/html/Chapter5.htm

Networked Digital Library of Theses and Dissertations (NDLTD). (n.d.). *History, description, and scope.* Retrieved August 13, 2004, from http://www.ndltd.org/info/description.en.html

Nims, J. K. (1999). Marketing library instruction services: Changes and trends. *Reference Services Review, 27*(3), 249–253. Retrieved August 22, 2004 from *Emerald FullText* database.

Online Computer Library Center. (2002, June). *Information habits of college students: How academic librarians can influence students' Web-based information choices.* (White paper). Retrieved August 13, 2004, from http://www5.oclc.org/downloads/community/informationhabits.pdf

Odlyzko, A. M. (1995). Tragic loss or good riddance? The impending demise of traditional scholarly journals. *International Journal of Human Computer Studies, 42,* 71–122.

Organization for Economic Co-operation and Development. (2002). *Households with access to the Internet, 2000 and 2001.* Retrieved August 13, 2004, from http://www.oecd.org/dataoecd/43/27/2766843.xls

Pace, A. K. (2003). *The ultimate digital library: Where the new information players meet.* Chicago: American Library Association.

Palloff, R. M., & Pratt, K. (2003). *The virtual student: A profile and guide to working with online learners.* San Francisco: Jossey-Bass.

Pew Internet & American Life Project. (2002, September 15). *The Internet goes to college: How students are living in the future with today's technology.* Retrieved August 13, 2004, from http://www.pewinternet.org/pdfs/PIP_College_Report.pdf

Pew Internet & American Life Project. (2004, August 11). *The Internet and daily life: Many Americans use the Internet in everyday activities, but traditional offline habits still dominate.* Retrieved November 28, 2004, from http://www.pewinternet.org/pdfs/PIP_Internet_and_Daily_Life.pdf

Prensky, M. (2001). Digital natives, digital immigrants. *On the Horizon, 9*(5). Retrieved August 13, 2004, from http://www.twitchspeed.com/site/Prensky%20-%20Digital%20Natives,%20Digital%20Immigrants%20-%20Part1.htm

Robins, D. (2002). From virtual libraries to digital libraries: The role of digital libraries in information communities. In C. F. Thomas (Ed.), *Libraries, the Internet, and scholarship* (pp. 45–75). New York: Marcel Dekker.

Rocklin, T. (2001). New developments in the learning environment: A partnership in faculty development. In B. I. Dewey (Ed.), *Library user education: Powerful learning, powerful partnerships* (pp. 53–60). Lanham, MD: Scarecrow Press.

Rockman, I. F. (2002, Fall). Strengthening connections between information literacy, general education, and assessment efforts. *Library Trends, 51*(2), 185–198.

Rockman, I. F. (2004). Introduction: The importance of information literacy. In I. F. Rockman (Ed.), *Integrating information literacy into the higher education curriculum: Practical models for transformation* (pp. 1–28). San Francisco: Jossey-Bass.

Roel, E. (2004). Electronic journal publication: A new library contribution to scholarly communication. *College & Research Libraries News, 65*(1): 23–26.

Rothenberg, D. (1998). How the Web destroys student research papers. *Education Digest, 63*(6), 59–61. Retrieved August 13, 2004, from *Academic Search Premier* database.

Scanlon, P. M. (2003). Student online plagiarism. *College Teaching, 51*(4), 161–165. Retrieved August 13, 2004, from *Academic Search Premier* database.

Schwartz, L., Clark, S., Cossarin, M., & Rudolph, J. (2004). Educational wikis: Features and selection criteria. *International Review of Research in Open and Distance Learning, 5*(1). Retrieved December 13, 2004, from http://www.irrodl.org/content/v5.1/technote_xxvii.html

Sever, I. (1994). Electronic information retrieval as culture shock: An anthropological exploration. *RQ, 33,* 336–341.

Sherman, C., & Price, G. (2001). *The invisible Web: Uncovering information sources search engines can't see.* Medford, NJ: Information Today. [Retrieved August 13, 2004, from companion Web site http://invisible-web.net/].

Slade, A. L., & Kascus, M. A. (2000). *Library services for open and distance learning: The third annotated bibliography.* Englewood, CO: Libraries Unlimited.

Smith Macklin, A. (2003, November). Theory into practice: Applying David Jonassen's work in instructional design to instruction programs in academic libraries. *College & Research Libraries, 64*(6), 494–500.

Starkweather, W. M., and Wallin, C. C. (1999, Spring). Faculty response to library technology: Insights on attitudes. *Library Trends, 47*(4), 640–668. Retrieved March 24, 2005, from *Academic Search Premier* database.

Sugarman, T. S., & Demetracopoulos, C. (2001). Creating a Web research guide: Collaboration between liaisons, faculty, and students. *Reference Services Review, 29*(2), 150–156.

Sullivan, D. (2004, November 18). *Google Scholar offers access to academic information.* Retrieved December 29, 2004, from http://searchenginewatch.com/searchday/article.php/3437471

University of California eScholarship Repository. (n.d.). *About the repository.* Retrieved August 16, 2004, from http://repositories.cdlib.org/escholarship/about.html

University of Waikato. (2000). *New Zealand Digital Library.* Retrieved August 13, 2004, from http://www.nzdl.org/fast-cgi-bin/library?a=p&p=home

Ury, C. J., Meldrem, J. A., & Johnson, C. V. (2000). Academic library outreach through faculty partnerships and Web-based research aids. In W. Arant & P. A. Mosley (Eds.), *Library outreach, partnerships, and distance education: Reference librarians at the Gateway* (pp. 243–256). Binghamton, NY: Haworth Press.

Van House, N. A., Bishop, A. P., & Buttenfield, B. P. (2003). Introduction: Digital libraries as sociotechnical systems. In A. P. Bishop, N. A. Van House, & B. P. Buttenfield (Eds.), *Digital library use: Social practice in design and evaluation* (pp. 1–21). Cambridge, MA: MIT Press.

Van Vuren, A. J., & Henning, J. C. (2001). User education in a flexible learning environment: An opportunity to stay relevant in the 21st century. *South African Journal of Library & Information Science, 67*(2), 79ff. Retrieved August 22, 2004, from *Academic Search Premier* database.

Vonnegut, K. (1985). *Galapagos.* New York: Delacorte Press.

Westney (Hattendorf), L. C. (2004). Mutually exclusive? Information technology in the tenure, promotion, and review process (pp. 30–43). In D. L. Andersen (Ed.), *Digital scholarship in the tenure, promotion, and review process.* Armonk, NY: Sharpe.

Wikipedia. (2004). *Wikipedia, the free encyclopedia.* Retrieved February 2, 2005, from http://en.wikipedia.org/wiki/Wiki

Wiley, D. A. (2000). Connecting learning objects to instructional design theory: A definition, a metaphor, and a taxonomy. In D. A. Wiley (Ed.), *The instructional use of learning objects.* [Online version]. Retrieved August 13, 2004, from http://www.reusability.org/read/

Wilson, B. (2000, September). The Lone Ranger is dead: Success today demands collaboration. *C&RL News, 61*(8), 698–701.

Wilson, L. A. (2001). Information literacy: Fluency across and beyond the university. In B. I. Dewey (Ed.), *Library user education: Powerful learning, powerful partnerships* (pp. 1–17). Lanham, MD: Scarecrow Press.

Zeidberg, D. S. (1999). The archival view of technology: Resources for the scholar of the future. *Library Trends, 47*(4), 796–805.

Index

Asterisks, 76

Athabasca University, 24, 25, 26; conference sessions at, 46; course development at, 39; Digital Reading Room case study at, 111–120; distance education sites at, 34–35; faculty-librarian collaboration at, 90; help sheets at, 42; information literacy case study at, 101–110; Internet resources of, 38; research guides at, 101–110

Audience, 82

Authentication, 72

Authority, 14

Authorship, 29, 82

AvantGo software, 124

B

Bailey, C. W., 31

Baird, C. M., 96

Bazaar Online Conference System, 25

Behr, M. D., 53

Bennett, J., 44, 45, 47

Bennett, L., 44, 45, 47

Bergman, M. K., 84*e*

Berkeley Digital Library SunSITE collections, 25

Berkeley Libraries, 42

Berners-Lee, T., 131, 132

Bibliographic instruction, 41

BioMed Central, 26

Bishop, A. P., 123

Blackboard, 25

Blackwell Synergy, 72

Blogging, 65

Bodleian Library Broadside Ballads collection, 80*e*

Boening, C. H., 82

Bontenbal, K. F., 60

Boole, G., 74

Boolean searches, 41, 53, 74–75

Borgman, C. L., 7, 15, 16, 30, 122, 123

Branding, 97

Breivik, P. S., 49, 54, 63

BrightPlanet, 84*e*

British Library, 4

Brod, C., 13

Browsing, 45, 76–77

Bruin Success with Less Stress tutorial, 56

Bush, V., 3

Buttenfield, B. P., 123

C

California Digital Library (CDL), 4, 5*e*, 128

California State University, 61–62, 63

Campus Alberta Repository of Educational Objects (CAREO), 118

Canadian Core Learning Resource Metadata Application Profile (CanCore), 119

Canadian Library Association, 98

Canadian Universities Reciprocal Borrowing Agreement, 43

Card catalogues, 3

Cassner, M., 97, 98

Cawthorne, J. E., 99

CDL. *See* California Digital Library (CDL)

Central Missouri State University, 39

Change, 13, 44–45

Chat reference, 41–42

Chowdhury, G. G., 4, 11, 124, 125

Chowdhury, S., 4, 11

CINAHL (Cumulative Index to Nursing & Allied Literature), 71

Citation styles, 86

CogPrints, 23

Collaboration: and culture, 53; for information literacy integration, 57, 59, 61. *See also* Faculty-librarian collaboration

Collaborative learning communities, 91

Collection development, 92–94

Communication: in distance education, 36, 37*f*; in faculty-librarian collaboration, 95

Computers, 122–126

Conference boards, 58, 96

Conferences, 46

Contact information, 35–36

Controlled vocabulary searching, 77

Conversagent technology, 131

Convey, J., 74

Cook, D., 91, 95, 99

Copyright agreements, 30, 87–88, 112

Cornell University, 129

Council on Library and Information Resources, 79

Course Authors Guide (Athabasca University), 39

Course development: at Athabasca University, 39; change of resources in, 33; and faculty development, 45–47; faculty-librarian collaboration for, 90, 95; and information literacy, 51, 55–64; and learning styles, 43–44; and librarians, 39–40; overview of, 38–39

Course reserve lists, 59

Course revision process, 67

Crash Course in Copyright, 87–88

Create Change, 27, 28

Creative Commons, 24–25

Creativity, 92

CrossRef, 127–128

Culture, 11, 53. *See also* Digital library culture

Cumulative Index to Nursing & Allied Literature. See CINAHL

Cuneiform Digital Library Initiative, 4, 5*e*

CUNY Bilingual Information Competency Tutorial, 56–57

Currency, 82

Curriculum development, 92

Currie, C. L., 36–37, 60

Curzon, S. C., 61

Customer service software, 131

D

Databases: functionality of, 123; help sheets for, 42; library users' familiarity with, 12; number of, 71; query formation for, 73–77; search features of, 127–132; search screens of, 73; search skills for, 70; search steps for, 70–78; services of, 21; trial availability of, 47; user-friendly searches of, 127–132

Deep Web, 84*e*

Dehumanization, 13

Delos Network of Excellence on Digital Libraries, 4

Demetracopoulos, T. M., 44, 58, 95

Departmental meetings, 97–98

Desktop computers, 122–126

Dialog, 71

Dictionaries, 71

Digital culture: characteristics of, 14–17; definition of, 3; and faculty, 29–31; and faculty development, 46–47; feelings related to, 11; and scholarly communication, 29–31

Digital divide, 2–3

Digital libraries: benefits of, 8–9; challenges of, 41, 85; contact information for, 35–36; current state of, 121–122; definition of, 7–8; descriptions of various, 4–7; in distance education courses, 35–38; ethics involving, 85–88; and faculty-librarian collaboration, 91; higher education's use of, 78–88; history of, 3–4; language of, 12–13; limitations of, 84–85; pace of

30–31; ethics involving, 85–88; higher education's use of, 78–88; limitations of, 84–85; scholars' recommendations of, 20–21; value of, versus print publications, 29–30

Electronic-Archiving Initiative, 28

Elloumi, F., 25

E-mail, 21, 41–42

Embedded assessment, 64

Encyclopedia Britannica, 108

Encyclopedias, 71

EndNote, 86

Enriching Scholarship program, 46

Enrollment, in college, 54

Error handling, 123

Ethics, 85–88

ETS. *See* Educational Testing Service (ETS)

Evaluation, of information: in Athabasca University research guides, 104; of database search results, 77–78; importance of, 53–54; on Internet, 82–83; need for, 54–55

Ex Libris, 127, 128

Expanded Academic ASAP, 71

F

Faculty: banning of Internet resources by, 37; and barriers to information literacy, 62–63; comfort of, with digital technology, 45; and digital culture, 29–31; digital technology concerns of, 79; digital technology's relationship to, 20–21; and distance education resources, 34, 38; distance education role of, 36; electronic publication use of, 79; information literacy integration role of, 55–59; librarians' relationship to, 20; resistance of, to change, 44–45

Faculty development, 44–47, 63

Faculty-librarian collaboration: in Athabasca University information literacy project, 101–102; in collection development, 92–94; communication in, 95; and course development, 90, 95; in Digital Reading Room case study, 111–120; and information literacy, 91–92; for integration of information literacy, 57, 59, 61; leadership in, 92; in marketing efforts, 96–98; and organizational climate, 98–99; overview of, 90–92; to promote research skills, 108–109; for research guides, 97; and teaching, 94–95. *See also* Collaboration

Fair dealing, 87

FAQs, 35

Feedback functions, 129–130

Field searching, 76

Finding Information page (Berkeley Libraries), 42

Flexibility, 15

Florida International University, 63

Foo, S., 124, 125

Forums, 58

Francoeur, S., 42

Friedlander, A., 79

Frustration, 1

Functionality, 123

G

Gaide, S., 97

Gale Directory of Online, Portable, and Internet Databases, 71

Gandhi, S., 93, 95

Gapen, D. K., 7

Gee, E. G., 49, 54, 63

GEMS (Gateway to Electronic Media Services), 129

vancement of Academic Publication
(ICAAP), 26
International Council for Open and Distance Education, 10
International Federation of Library Associations and Institutions (IFLA), 66
International Review of Research in Open and Distance Learning (IRRODL), 26
International students, 44
Internet: digital library history role of, 3–4; distance education resources on, 34, 38; and dumbing down of work, 81; ethics involving, 85–88; evaluation of information on, 82–83; faculty's ban of resources from, 37; goal of research on, 54; increased use of, 2; limitations of, 84–85; number of students using, 81; problem with sources cited on, 82–83; quality of resources on, 37, 82; resources listing of, 135–140; scholarly communication role of, 21–22; sharing information on, 24–29
Invisible Web, 83, 84*e*
IRRODL. See International Review of Research in Open and Distance Learning (IRRODL)
ISI Web of Knowledge, 71
Isolation, 13, 35

J

Jargon, 12
Jeffries, S., 95, 97
John, N. R., 124
Johns Hopkins University Press, 29
Johnson, C. V., 39, 46–47
Johnson, K., 20, 116
Journal of Insect Science, 28
Journal of Library & Information Services in Distance Education (Mikesell), 93
Journal subscriptions: and collection de-

velopment, 93; and database searches, 72–73; rising cost of, 27, 29; students' perception of, 37
Journaling, 65
Journals. *See* Electronic journals
JSTOR, 28–29, 71

K

Kascus, M., 10
Kelley, K. B., 41, 96
Kennedy, D., 91, 95
Kennedy, S., 84
Kent State University, 66
Kling, R., 30
Knowledge, 54–55
Kupersmith, J., 13–14

L

LaGuardia, C., 93
Language, 11–13
Large, A., 77
Lassila, O., 132
Leadership, 92
Learner-centered classrooms, 36, 37*f*, 60
Learning objects, 117–120
Learning styles, 43–44
Learning Technology Standards Committee (LTSC), 117
Leighton, D., 126
LexisNexis, 71
Librarian-faculty collaboration. *See* Faculty-librarian collaboration
Librarians: acculturation role of, 17; changing role of, 91; and course development, 39–40; digital library history role of, 3–4; digital scholarship roles of, 132–133; and distance education challenges, 40; future of, 10–11; instructional roles of, 94, 95; and integration of information literacy, 56–59;

language of, 11, 12; relationship of users to, 20; role of, in academic libraries, 10; support of open access from, 27; tasks of, in digital library promotion, 35–36; and tutorial challenges, 53

Libraries: history of, 122; integration of digital technology in, 11; traditional role of, 3. *See also specific types*

Library and Archives Canada, 38

Library building, 14

Library catalogues, 127

Library Journal (LaGuardia), 93

Library of Congress, 4, 6

Library practica, 65

Library searches: in academic versus digital libraries, 40–41; classes in, 52–53; expansion of skills in, 52, 53–54; faculty development in, 46–47; increased access points in, 52; and interface design, 123; steps for database searches in, 70–78; students' submission of strategies for, 57; user-friendliness of, 126–132; varying skills sets for, 70

Licensing agreements: in academic libraries, 10; and accessibility, 15; and database searches, 72; and online sharing, 24–25; and publication recommendations, 20

Licklider, J.C.R., 3

Lillard, L. L., 39, 96

Lindsay, N. K., 45

Link servers, 127–129

Links by Subject

Literature Online database, 35

Literature reviews, 65

Littlejohn, A., 117

Live Assistance, 41

LivePerson software, 41, 131

Loan periods, 112

Longevity, 15–16

Lowe, C. A., 49, 50

LTSC. *See* Learning Technology Standards Committee (LTSC)

Lund University Libraries, 26

Lynch, C., 21, 124

Lynch, L., 15, 24

M

Machine-readable cataloguing format (MARC), 3

Marketing, 35, 96–98

Master of Arts Integrated Studies (MAIS) program, 105–106, 116

Mattison, D., 125

McKim, G., 30

MEDLINE, 73

Meldrem, J. A., 39, 46–47

Menus, 13

MERLIN tutorial, 56

MERLOT. *See* Multimedia Educational Resource for Learning and Online Teaching (MERLOT)

Meszaros, R. L., 22

MetaCrawler, 128

Metadata, 12–13, 119

MetaFind, 128

MetaLib, 128

Meyyappan, N., 124, 125

Middle States Commission on Higher Education (MSCHE), 50, 51–52, 59, 62, 66, 67, 91

Mikesell, B., 93

Millennium AirPAC, 124

Milton S. Eisenhower Library, 29

Mission statements, 61–62

MIT Libraries, 16

MIT OpenCourseWare resource, 25

Moisey, S., 120

Moodle, 25

Mouat, J., 108
Moveable type, 21
MSCHE. *See* Middle States Commission on Higher Education (MSCHE)
Multimedia Educational Resource for Learning and Online Teaching (MERLOT), 118
MyLibrary, 129
myNTU, 129

N

Nanyang Technological University, 124–125, 129
National Center for Education Statistics, 9–10
National Higher Education ICT Initiative, 66
National Telecommunications and Information Administration, 2
Natural language processing, 130–131
Nesting, 75–76
Netiquette, 87
Networked Digital Library of Theses and Dissertations (NDLTD), 23
New Zealand Digital Library, 4, 6e
Newsletters, 35, 97
Nichols, D., 45, 46
Nims, J. K., 96
Nineteenth-Century Art Worldwide (NCAW), 26
Not-for-profit publishers, 28

O

Odlyzko, A. M., 27
Online bookstores, 126–127
Online Computer Library Center, 81–82
Online Medieval and Classical Library, 25
Online public access catalogues (OPACs), 3
Open access journals, 26–27
Open University, 38, 131

Organization, 82
Organization for Economic Co-operation and Development, 2
Organizational climate, 98–99
Orr, G. J., 41, 96
Outcomes-based assessment, 64
Ownership, 10, 29
Oxford English Dictionary Online, 108
Oxford Reference Online, 71
OYEZ Project, 24

P

Pace, A. K., 27, 85, 126
Pace University Library, 126
PageRank technology, 78
Palloff, R. M., 55
Palm handheld devices, 123–124
Pay-per-view options, 21
PDA Zone, 124
Peer review, 27, 28
Penn State Libraries Online Reference Resources, 38
Personal use areas, 21
Personality, 16
Personalized digital library environments, 129
Perspective, 82
Pew Internet & American Life Project, 2, 81
Phrase searching, 75
Physical Sciences Information Gateway. *See* PSIgate
Plagiarism, 85–88
Plagiarism & Academic Integrity at Rutgers University, 86
Pratt, K., 55
Precision, 77
Prensky, M., 81
Preprints, 30
Preservation, 16, 28–29

Slade, A., 10

SmarterChild, 131

Smith Macklin, A., 37

Social Sciences Citation Index, 71

Social scientists, 31

Sociological Abstracts, 71

SOSIG (Social Science Information Gateway), 83

SPARC. *See* Scholarly Publishing and Academic Resources Coalition (SPARC)

Spitzer, K. L., 49, 50

Spradling, C., 46–47

Standards statements, 61–62

Starkweather, W. M., 45

Statistical databases, 71

Statistical Universe, 71

Storage, 15–16

Students: digital technology's relationship to, 20–21; electronic publication recommendations of, 20–21; electronic publication use of, 81–84; expectations of digital libraries by, 54; factors affecting resource use of, 36–37; learning styles, 43–44; librarians' relationship to, 20; number of, using Internet, 81; perception of subscriptions by, 37; submission of search strategies by, 57; technology proficiency of, 52

Style, 82

Subject Portals, 38

Sugarman, T. S., 44, 58, 95

Sullivan, D., 84

Sutch, L., 45, 46

Synonyms, 74

T

Teacher-centered classrooms, 36

Teaching: change of resources in, 33; digital libraries in, 35–38; and faculty-librarian collaboration, 94–95; and information literacy, 51, 55–64

Teaching and Learning with Technology Conference, 46

The Teaching Librarian (Francoeur), 42

Technostress, 13–14

Tedd, L. A., 77

Tenure, 45

THOMAS, 6

TILT tutorial, 56

Time, 45

Tin, T., 20, 116

Tone, 82

Trabelsi, H., 20

Truncation, 76

Trustworthiness, 30

Tucker, D. C., 124

Tutorials: challenges of, 53; and challenges of distance education, 41; and integration of information literacy, 56–57; in library promotions, 35

24/7 Reference software, 131

U

UK's Routes, 38

Ulrich's Periodicals Directory, 26

University College Dublin, 38

University of Alberta, 124

University of Arizona, 28

University of California, 80*e*

University of California eScholarship Repository, 22

University of California Irvine Libraries, 42

University of Louisville, 63–64

University of Maryland University College, 42

University of Massachusetts Amherst, 64

University of Michigan, 46

University of Oxford, 80*e*

University of Southern California, 46
University of Texas at Austin, 80*e*
University of Toronto, 80*e*
University of Wisconsin, 118
Upstream model, 124
Ury, C. J., 39
U.S. Supreme Court, 24

V

Van House, N. A., 123
Van Vuren, A. J., 56
Virtual communities, 55
Vonnegut, K., 1

W

Wallin, C. C., 45
Washington State Assessment of Information and Technology Literacy, 65–66
Web development, 95
Web tutorials. *See* Tutorials
Web-based instructional units, 59
WebCT, 25, 40
Westney, L. C., 30
What Would a Batgirl Do? (Winnipeg Library & Information Services), 125
Wikipedia, 125

Wikis, 125
Wild cards, 76
Wiley, D., 117
Williams, P. B., 45
Wilson, B., 99
Wilson, L. A., 55, 96
Wilson OmniFile, 71
Winnipeg Library & Information Services, 125
Wireless devices, 123–124
Wisconsin Online Resource Center, 118
WoPEc, 23
World Wide Learn, 10

X

xreferplus, 71

Y

You Quote It, You Note It (Acadia University), 86

Z

Zeidberg, D. S., 15
Z39.50 Gateway, 129
Zurkowski, P., 49